An Essay on
ECONOMIC GROWTH
AND PLANNING

An Essay on
ECONOMIC GROWTH
AND PLANNING

by
MAURICE DOBB
M.A., Lecturer and Fellow of Trinity College, Cambridge

MODERN READER PAPERBACKS
NEW YORK AND LONDON

ISBN 978-0-85345-117-4 (pbk.)

Monthly Review Press
146 W. 29th Street, Suite 6W
New York, NY 10001

CONTENTS

v

PREFACE

INSTEAD of being called an Essay, this could, I suppose, have been called Lectures, since much of it has formed the substance of lectures, in Cambridge and elsewhere, during the past few years. Not all of it has, however, and at any rate none in quite its present shape. With the possible exception of the last chapter, it is more concerned with ways of thinking about economic growth than with actual policies and events. Nevertheless it will be seen (I hope) to be fairly closely related to actual problems of development and of planning; and I think it may serve to show many of the textbook-maxims about growth that have been current in the past to be inadequate, to say the least.

In a sphere where so many and such eminent voices have spoken in the past decade or two it is not easy to make specific acknowledgements. At an early stage the author had the benefit of discussion of these matters with Mr. R. M. Goodwin and Professor H. G. Johnson. Dr. Amartya Kumar Sen, whose ideas have in some respects developed along parallel lines to my own, is acknowledged below in relevant parts of the text. He was good enough to read and discuss more than one draft of this Essay. I owe a special debt to Dr. A. Ghosh of the Department of Applied Economics at Cambridge and Mr. Leif Johansen of the University of Oslo who spared time and thought from the preoccupations of their own work to check some of the formulations in the text and to compose the two mathematical notes to Chapters III and IV which stand in their names.

Cambridge, May 1959   M. H. D.

I

PLANNING

ALTHOUGH the recent revival of interest among economists
in questions of economic growth seems to have derived on
the formal side from the study of fluctuations and of the relation between fluctuation and trend, it has undoubtedly been
stimulated from the practical side by discussion of the development plans of underdeveloped countries and of comparative
growth-rates in the capitalist and socialist sectors of the world.
Yet the theories of economic growth recently in vogue among
economists have been concerned almost exclusively with growth
in capitalist economies where capital is in private ownership and
investment predominantly under the control of private individuals or firms.* Little or no attention seems so far to have been
paid to the question whether or not their relevance is restricted
to these institutional assumptions. Do such theories have a more
universal application; if so in what form; if not, what alternative
approach is proper to analysing problems of growth in a planned
economy where capital is socially owned and hence investment
is (in some sense) socially controlled? This is a question that
seems worth asking, and to do so is the purpose of this essay.

* Mr. Harrod, for instance, assumes that "growth is the aggregated effect of a
great number of individual decisions" (*Towards a Dynamic Economics*, London 1948,
pp. 76–7); and his "warranted rate of growth" expresses "the equilibrium of a
steady advance" in the sense of "the condition in which producers will be content
with what they are doing." In Mrs. Joan Robinson's *Accumulation of Capital* (London, 1956) this reference is, of course, explicit: *vide* the frequent mention of what
happens under "the capitalist rules of the game". Mr. Kaldor's model (*Economic
Journal*, Dec. 1957), makes a similar explicit reference (pp. 591–3, 618); although
there is a hint (no more) that it may hold lessons in a wider context than this.

Since these theories, deriving as they largely do from the well-known Harrod and Domar growth-conditions, follow the Keynesian tradition in focusing attention upon the savings-investment relation, or income-expenditure balance, there might seem to be a crucial reason why they should have no application to a socialist economy: namely, that in the latter there is an identity of savings-decisions and investment-decisions, not a separation of them (in so far at any rate as investment is 'financed' from the incomes of State institutions and not from the savings of private individuals). Certain corollaries of these theories, however, have been applied to the development plans of under-developed countries in the form of criteria for investment policy —criteria as to what the social interest requires that investment *should* be, as distinct from statements of what it *tends* to be. One such corollary, to the effect that investment should generally choose the (technical) form that minimizes the capital-output ratio, we shall consider later on. It might be as well accordingly to start by setting out the more obvious ways in which the *modus operandi* of a planned economy is likely to differ from that of an unplanned capitalist economy.

Firstly, investment in a planned economy is presumably determined as a policy-decision of the government, and not as the resultant of market forces which the government may seek to influence by playing upon investment-incentives or *via* monetary policy but does not control directly. This applies to the total amount (or rate) of investment, its distribution between economic sectors (also probably between individual industries within each sector) and (in the main) the technical forms in which investment is embodied. In taking decisions about the allocation of labour and resources between the production of capital goods and the production of consumer goods, it will be taking *ipso facto* a 'savings'-decision; and expressed in real terms both 'investment' and 'saving' must refer to the surplus of total production (gross or net), over that part of production that is destined for current consumption. (Things can only look different from the production angle from what they do from the consumers' end of the process if there is a change in stocks of goods-in-process or of goods that have passed off the production-line but not yet into use.) Once, however, we introduce exchange and with it the prices of actual exchange transactions, we can classify income and expenditure separately and give a meaning to the savings-ratio that makes the two ratios no longer identical. Thus 'savings' can be defined as the difference between the incomes (in money) of both private persons and State institutions* and expenditures within the given period upon purchase of consumer goods. This need not at any time be the same as the amount that the State is currently spending on capital goods of all kinds (at cost), even if we ignore expenditure by the State on the provision of free services (e.g. health, education). In the absence of savings out of personal incomes and of any purchases of consumer goods by State institutions, saving thus defined becomes equivalent to the total income of State institutions; and any statement about equality between saving and investment as an equilibrium condition could be thought of as pertaining exclusively to State book-keeping: as being a statement about the balance in money terms of State receipts and expenditures. Since there is no obvious reason why the State's money receipts and expenditures should balance, this is perhaps too formal a way of putting it. What is of more substantial importance is the price-level of consumer goods in relation to the level of costs (which in the last analysis depends upon the level of wages from which personal incomes are derived). This relation will be a crucial determinant of the income of State institutions; and accordingly any economic significance that equality between saving and investment may have must have reference to this price-relation. On this matter we shall have something more to say in the final chapter. What deserves emphasis here is that such a condition refers exclusively to the price-relations of this type of economy, and does not extend to real or production-relations (or structural relations in production as I should prefer to call them to avoid a possible ambiguity).

One qualification should perhaps be made explicit here.

---

* State income would presumably be defined so as to exclude taxes on personal incomes if the latter were reckoned pre-tax. Taxes on State institutions represent a transfer of income from one department of State to another, and would have to be treated so as to avoid double counting: i.e., excise duty or turnover tax would be counted as a revenue if it had not previously been calculated as part of the net income of industrial or trading organizations, but a tax on profit would *not* be counted if the profits of industrial and trading enterprises had been calculated pre-tax.

What has just been said will apply if investment decisions are centrally planned. It is possible, however, that a socialist economy could operate a decentralized mechanism for the determination of investment policy, whereby State enterprises made their investment plans as independent units according to some profit-criterion, as was suggested by certain participants in the pre-war economists' debate about price-policy under socialism (or *wirtschaftsrechnung*) and as operates to some extent, in principle at least, in Yugoslavia today. Such a criterion might be either the profit to be *expected* in the future as a result of making the investment or the profit actually realized on past activities (and determining the funds at the disposal of the enterprise in question). In such a situation the amount of actual constructional activity in progress, and hence the demand for and output of capital goods, will *not* be independent of price-relations, but will be influenced by the latter *via* the incomes of enterprises. A multiplier relation will exist between any initial change in investment which changes the incomes of enterprises (*via* a change in wages or employment or *via* a change in the price or the sales of capital goods) and subsequent expenditures of enterprises on further investment. Thereby an Harrodian cumulative tendency may be set up, and one that could be even greater than in a capitalist economy to the extent that investment by State industries depends upon the funds at their disposal and, since no profits are distributed to rich shareholders, profits are seldom 'saved'.* (In this context, taxation of the profits of enterprises is, of course, equivalent to saving, and the more they are taxed the smaller will this multiplier-effect be.) Even if all fixed investment is centrally planned, some tendency of this kind may operate, in the degree to which the managements of enterprises have discretion as to the amount of stocks they hold (i.e. stocks of materials or fuel or semi-finished products)—and they are bound to have considerable discretion *de facto* even under the most centralized planning.† In other words, the qualification is

---

* Cf. the present writer's 'Saving and Investment in a Socialist Economy' in *Economic Journal*, Dec. 1939, p. 721.

† *Vide* the constant problem this presented and the various attempts to limit it by credit control in the Soviet experience (cf. the present writer's *Soviet Economic Development since 1917*, pp. 356, 382, and Dr. R. W. Davies, *The Development of the Soviet Budgetary System* (Cambridge, 1958), pp. 158, 231).

important to the extent that the amount of real investment is susceptible to influence by the market.

A second and very obvious contrast between a planned and an unplanned system is that there will be no need in the former for the rate of investment to be governed by the time-preferences of individual savers (as indeed is already so under capitalism to the extent that the rate of investment is directly influenced by monetary policy). Some economists, however, have maintained that it ought to be so limited if economic welfare is to be maximized—at any rate, once sufficient investment is being currently undertaken for full employment to be maintained. This is a matter to which we shall return in Chapter II.

Thirdly, there is similarly no need for the technical form of investment to be decided by what is the most profitable form— although here again there will be a tendency for this to be a decisive factor so far as discretion is left to the enterprise regarding choice of technique. It is a question deserving some attention whether any of the criteria that have been discussed by economists in recent years amounts to the same thing as choosing the most profitable technique, and which of them is the right one. On this we shall have some more to say in the sequel.

Fourthly, there is a contrast in the mode of determining the allocation of investment between various sectors of the economy which may make a crucial difference to the development path which that economy pursues, to its speed of movement along that path, perhaps also to the very possibility of certain kinds of development and in some circumstances to the possibility of any development at all. Instead of the allocation-pattern of investment being a product in the first instance of the guesses and expectations of a large number of independent decision-takers (*entrepreneurs*), in the long run 'revised' by *ex post* movements of market prices, economic planning essentially consists of an attempt to secure a co-ordinated set of investment-decisions *ex ante* —in advance of any commitment of resources to particular constructional projects or installations. The difference is both real and important for two main reasons: firstly, because fixed investment is concerned with crystallizing labour and resources in durable forms, so that once this has been undertaken the process of 'revision' of initial decisions by subsequent shifts in market prices can operate only after a considerable lapse of time;

secondly, since current investment by changing both productive
capacity and employment can exercise an important influence
upon market prices (an influence that is likely to be the greater
over any period the larger is new investment over that period
as a ratio to the existing stock of capital equipment.) Accordingly the existing structure of market prices cannot be taken as
a sure basis for forecasting what the future structure, and hence
the return on any particular investment project, will be.

This is a theme on which the present writer has harped a good
deal on other occasions, and he will try to restrain any inclina-
tion to enlarge upon it here. For the sake of clarity, however,
one or two things must be briefly said. Recent discussion of the
problems of underdeveloped countries, and especially the work
of Professor Nurkse, has given renewed emphasis to the notion
of external economies,* in the shape of the influence of the
development of one industry or sector upon the possibilities of
development in others: for example, of the development of
transport or of sources of fuel and power upon both the costs
and the market possibilities of diverse manufacturing industries,
or of an engineering industry upon the growth-potentiality of
industry in general. In their original context of the analysis of
static equilibrium, the existence of external economies (or diseconomies) was treated as a reason for a divergence between the
equilibrium allocation of resources dictated by the profit-moti-
vation of individual firms and that dictated by the general social
advantage; and they were apt to be thought of as economies
accruing to other firms *within* a given industry, rather than as
economies accruing to other industries from a given change in
the output of any one. When the matter is placed in the context
of development, the whole notion acquires both a wider and
more crucial significance as something integral to the process of
growth; as a necessary condition for growth to occur, and not
just an incidental factor that happens to be ignored in the
market-equilibrating process.† It appears as nothing less than

* Nurkse, *Problems of Capital Formation in Underdeveloped Countries* (Oxford, 1953),
pp. 6–10, 14–15, 27.
† Cf. T. Scitovsky, 'Two Concepts of External Economies' in *Journal of Political
Economy*, April 1954, p. 143: "External economies as defined in the theory of industrialization include, but go far beyond, the external economies of equilibrium
theory." The former include interdependence between producers that operates
through the market (which he terms 'pecuniary external economies') as well as those

the interdependence of different elements in an organic process of growth: an interdependence that defines an essential balance without which growth may be impossible or if it starts may be quickly halted. Thus the growth-potentiality of the whole system will not be a simple sum of the growth-potentialities of its constituent sectors or industries separately viewed (with appropriate adjustments of scale): it will vary with the structural pattern according to which the system as a whole grows. Some structural patterns will be much more conducive to growth than others, and it may well be that in any given context one can speak of an optimum pattern of growth. An implicit premiss of this essay is that such structural relations in production are more worth-while as a focus of attention than the income-expenditure balance upon which attention has been mainly focused hitherto.*

At the core of the difference in this respect of which we have spoken between a planned economy and an atomistic market economy lies the factor of uncertainty. But it is uncertainty of a special kind. If each decision-taker in a market economy could estimate future prices on the basis of present prices (which we have seen that he cannot do), or if he could correctly estimate the investment-decisions being concurrently made by all other *entrepreneurs* throughout the system, and also those to be made at all future dates throughout the life-period of the concrete investment-project in question, the difference in question between the two economic mechanisms would disappear (with a qualification that we shall mention in a moment). Such knowledge the decision-takers cannot have unless there is sufficient collusion between them for them all both to pool knowledge of their intentions† and to allow for some adjustment of these intentions in the light of knowledge by each of the totality of intentions; which is equivalent to saying that some kind of plan

operating directly and not through the market, which are alone relevant to static equilibrium (in the absence of indivisibilities in production). Cf. also J. E. Meade, 'External Economies and Diseconomies in a Competitive Situation', in *Economic Journal*, March, 1952.

* Cf. on this the remarks of A. Lowe in *Capital Formation in Economic Growth* (Princeton, 1955), p. 585; and Ch. Bettelheim in *Revue Économique*, Jan. 1957, p. 5.

† This, however, would need to include, not only knowledge about each other's intentions with regard to *current* investment, but also with regard to investment at future dates.

emerges by the terms of which each individual (but no longer independent) decision-taker consents or is obliged to be bound.*

It is this kind of uncertainty to which Professor Koopmans is presumably referring when he speaks of "secondary uncertainty arising from lack of communication, that is from one decision-maker having no way of finding out the concurrent decisions and plans made by others". This he suggests "is quantitatively at least as important as the primary uncertainty arising from random acts of nature and unpredictable changes in consumers' preferences". To this he adds the statement that "dependence of one man's decision criterion on other men's decisions appears to leave no room for efficient price-guided allocation". †

If such uncertainty is sufficiently great, it may so inhibit investment decisions as to arrest growth entirely—or rather one should say (since one cannot separate uncertainty as an objective factor from the subjective attitude of *entrepreneurs* towards it) if this uncertainty and the caution or pessimism of *entrepreneurs* in face of it is sufficiently great. This is a familiar situation in underdeveloped countries.

For precisely the same reason, any change of development-path can be made more easily and at less cost in the degree to which it can be foreseen by the decision-takers and hence planned ahead. This will be the case whether the change is one in the location of industry or from a high to a low rate of investment, requiring a reduction in the size (relative and perhaps absolute) of the capital goods sector of industry, a change from war to peace or from an emphasis upon agriculture to an emphasis upon industry or from production for export to production for the home market. If development is occurring at a very high rate such shifts in the structural pattern of industry may involve no more than a relative shift of resources, and be absorbed by a marking-time in some industries while others continue to go forward. But in the more ordinary case (and *a fortiori*

* Cf. T. Scitovsky, *loc. cit.*, p. 149: "Only if expansion in the . . . industries were integrated and planned together would the profitability of investment in each of them be a reliable index of its social desirability. . . . Complete integration of all industries would be necessary to eliminate all divergence between private profit and public benefit [due to 'pecuniary external economies']."

† T. C. Koopmans, *Three Essays on the State of Economic Science*, pp. 154, 163; cf. also pp. 146–7. In a work of many years ago the present writer termed this "individualist uncertainty".

the shorter the notice at which the switch occurs) there will need to be an absolute transfer of labour and other resources, including capital equipment, from old lines of production to new. Because of the intractability of resources once they have taken the form of fixed capital, this cannot be done costlessly: the 'transfer' cannot be a *real* transfer, but must take the form of constructing new equipment for the expanding line of production and simultaneously under-utilizing or prematurely scrapping the equipment immobilized in older lines of production for which demand is now dwindling.* A social loss of this kind (consisting in the larger gross investment cost of maintaining a given flow of national income over any stretch of time, e.g. a decade) is bound to be involved if the process of changing direction is governed exclusively by the market, since the price-change which is the guide and signal to changed allocation of investment follows and does not precede the shift of demand. To the extent, however, that the shift can be anticipated and hence planned for in advance, this premature obsolescence of equipment can be avoided. Investment in fixed capital in the old line of production can be terminated or tapered off at an earlier date, so that this fixed capital is nearing the end of its physical life at the date in the future at which it is likely to be no longer required. In the meantime labour and equipment that in normal circumstances would be devoted to maintenance (or replacement) of this fixed capital, soon to become redundant, can be transferred to making and installing fixed capital in anticipation of the new and expanding use for it. It is sometimes contended that a planned economy would tend to introduce rigidity into the limbs of the economic system, rendering it more conservative and resistant to change than the more flexible mechanism of decentralized and market-guided decision. Such rigidity may well be a tendency of large bureaucratic administrative units, whether private or State. Why it should necessarily

---

* Of course, this social cost could alternatively be avoided if the change were forcibly prevented from occurring until fixed capital in the old line had reduced itself by natural processes of decay. But this would merely substitute for the social cost in question the social loss from retardation of desirable change. Nor is the former removed entirely (though it may be mitigated) by maintaining the old equipment in use as long as the demand for it suffices to enable it to operate at a price covering prime cost. The equipment will still be serving what is (from a long term view) an *inferior* use, and unless demand in this use is highly elastic it is likely to be scrapped before its 'normal' life-span is ended.

affect planning organizations, which could perhaps be expected
to have a bias towards experimentation and novelty, is not at all
clear (although it is doubtless true that over-centralized planning may stunt and fetter initiative at the lower levels of management). Be that as it may, however, such a contention, baldly
put as it commonly is, seems to overlook this countervailing
consideration of the enhanced *potentiality* of a planning mechanism for removing a leading obstacle to economic change which
the intractability of fixed capital imposes.

The incidence of this 'secondary uncertainty', however, is
unlikely to be spread evenly over all lines of production. In so
far as it affects some industries or sectors more strongly than
others, it will exert a bias upon the direction of investment and
hence upon the structural pattern of development, as well as
retarding the general rate of investment and begetting special
costs of unforeseen change. There is indeed every reason to expect this type of uncertainty to bear more heavily upon some
sectors than upon others, since the degree of uncertainty will be
a function of the remoteness in time of a given investment decision from the final demand which it is designed to serve or
from other sets of economic events which are its essential com-
plement; and this time-interval will depend *inter alia* on the
periods of construction and durability, which are likely to vary
considerably in different types of industry. When we take this
consideration into account we might seem to be faced with the
problem of explaining why economic development under Capitalism has proceeded even at the *tempo* and with as much coherence (or as little lack of coherence) as it has done in major
countries such as Britain, Germany and U.S.A. The answer
would seem to be that a market system is not without a means
whereby unbalanced development can produce its counter-
action, if tardily, in the shape of a rise in profitability (or expected profitability) in the neglected sectors of development;
this rise of profitability occurring as a result of the pent-up
demand generated by the expansion of the more developed
sectors. At some point prices and profits will rise to a level
sufficient to attract some investment to these previously neglected spheres despite the deterrent effect of the abnormal incidence
upon them of uncertainty. The process of development may be
uneven, discontinuous and wave-like, each wave associated with

a different kind of investment-peak, with a different point of concentration; but eventually some kind of coherent all-round advance may result. This is to assume, however, that investment in the more advanced sectors can and will be pushed ahead despite the absence of complementary developments elsewhere, and for a long enough time to accumulate the pressures needed to overcome the lag of the latter and to bring them into line. The very accumulation of these pressures (hingeing as it does on unsatisfied demand) will have a two-way influence, braking the advance of the sectors that have forged ahead as well as pulling at those that have lagged behind. It is far from certain that un-balanced development will in fact bring its correction through the market, even after an appreciable time-lag; the braking-effect may be stronger, or more quickly-acting, than the towing-effect; the resistance of reluctant sectors to being towed may undermine the initiative of the more venturesome; and the up-shot may simply be general retardation or stagnation.

Yet the whole of the difference of which we have spoken between the two economic mechanisms cannot be covered by the label of uncertainty. On the one hand, there are cases where, even in the absence of uncertainty (if this be conceiv-able), a decentralized market-mechanism would not achieve development: for example, where the expansion of one industry could not be undertaken at a profit, at least until an initial stage was passed, and yet its existence was essential to the growth of other industries, and without it these others would be brought to a standstill. This one might perhaps call the pure external economies case.* A leading reason for this is the existence of substantial indivisibilities of capital equipment; and the fact that these are likely to be significantly large (relatively to the

* It could be argued that if uncertainty were absent, this case could not arise unless the subsidy required to make the first industry pay exceeded what could be raised by a tax on the prospective profits of the other industries reliant on the first without reducing those profits below the minimum necessary to promote invest-ment (at some given rate); otherwise, in the absence of uncertainty the latter indus-tries, needing the products of the former, would bid up the price of these products at the expense of their own profits until that former ('infant') industry could pay its way. Accordingly the case reduces to one where the *social* rate of time-discount is lower than the individuals' time-discount (and hence the interest-rate). However, this seems to imply so refined a definition of 'absence of uncertainty' as to become rather absurd: it implies not merely the kind of collusion referred to above, but also knowledge of what a non-existent industry's output would be as well as knowledge by it of what price would be offered to it if it were to come into existence.

scale of the economy) at early stages of development gives this problem special prominence in underdeveloped countries.* Nurkse's example of Chile at once comes to mind, where "a modern rolling mill, which is standard equipment in any industrial country, can produce in three hours a sufficient supply of a certain type of iron shapes to last the country for a year. In these cases the inducement to instal such equipment is lacking."† There are other reasons, too: for example, the absence or backwardness of what it has become fashionable to call an 'infrastructure' for industrial growth. On the other hand, it is not *only* a matter of removing uncertainty by co-ordination of decisions; and the economic *rationale* of planning is not exhausted by mere co-ordination (such as comes simply from enlarging the size of the unit of decision). We have already said that the particular structural pattern adopted may significantly affect the *rate* of growth of the whole. A leading example of this with which we shall be concerned later is the structural relation between the sector of industries producing capital goods and the sector producing consumer goods. 'Co-ordination' may be on the basis of various structural patterns; and a form of planning that concerned itself *only* to achieve co-ordination and was neutral with regard to structural pattern could be considered as doing only half (perhaps less than half) its proper job.

What we have been saying does not rest on the pretence that this type of uncertainty is the only one—on a denial that Koopman's "primary uncertainty" exists. It is the latter, associated especially with the unknowns of technical discovery, possibly also those of population change and of human wants and the human contribution to labour productivity, that will set a time-horizon to any planning, since beyond a certain time-horizon these unknowns in the problem will become too large to make planning worth while, or at any rate, if plans are made, large enough to frustrate their achievement. It is true, however, that judgement as to the importance to be attached to such considerations as we have been speaking of will depend on one's

---

* Cf. W. Fellner, *Trends and Cycles in Economic Activity* (New York, 1956), pp. 199–200; where of this problem (associated with "complementarities among different sorts of specialized equipment", generally "the consequences of indivisibilities") it is said that it "may be of great significance for the understanding of conditions in primitive economies". Also cf. H. Leibenstein, *Economic Backwardness and Economic Growth* (New York, 1957), pp. 106–8.   † *Op. cit.*, p. 7.

estimate of the relative importance of the two kinds of uncertainty; since if the time-horizon of planning is very narrow,
it will operate always within a framework of fairly strict determinism, and apart from the effects of co-ordinating *current* decisions and the 'pure' external economies case it is likely (in so
far as it is realistic) simply to record as targets what would have
tended to happen in its absence. But it seems pretty evident that
investment policy can in most circumstances be postulated with
an adequate degree of realism for a quite substantial period
ahead, at any rate as regards macro-economic relations;* and
the further ahead one can plan, the wider the area of choice
and the greater the influence that planning can exercise upon
development. It is as well, however, to remember that this area
of choice *is* limited; there never exists more than a restricted
number of alternatives that can appear on a planning agenda;
and it may be at least as important to study realistically the
constraints upon investment policy in particular situations as to
discuss criteria for choosing between the limited number of
alternative policies than can be regarded as available.

What has just been said implies that there are two contrasted
methods of approach to analysing the investment problems of a
planned economy. Firstly, one can seek for some principle to
guide investment policy in choosing between various alternatives (as regards the rate of investment, the pattern of invest-
ment-distribution and its technical forms). Such a principle will
presumably be a maximizing principle, such as maximizing
utility or the social welfare of consumers over time, or possibly
minimizing something, such as expenditure of labour over time
to maintain a given output-flow. There are certain formal
difficulties about such theorems, since the result may be affected
by the period of time chosen for one's maximizing, and the
choice of period will be arbitrary. However, such formal difficulties are not, I believe, the most serious ones. More serious is
the difficulty of giving to such maximizing theorems any real
content. Were it not for this I see no reason to regard such an
approach as other than useful and important. Even if one could

---

* The fact is that there will be a series of time-horizons for different categories of
decision, not just one. For many micro-economic decisions, affecting particular
products, this horizon may be fairly narrow; but for broad strategic decisions
affecting the balance of the economy as a whole, or its transport-map and broad
locational pattern, it may extend over several decades.

never have any serious hope of attaining the best, such a principle would offer a standard for judging between practicable
alternatives (provided one knew what these were) in terms of
better and worse. I do not believe the view is tenable that, in
order to say which of two alternatives is the better, one has first
to define what one means by the best. This is not to say, however, that a clear idea of what is best cannot help one a great
deal in pronouncing about what is better. It seems to be as well,
therefore, to proceed by first saying something about this approach (which we shall do in the next chapter) and indicating
why it seems to lead one into a blind alley.

The second approach is to examine what are the key determining factors in growth which set limits to what a plan can
hope to do in any given situation—and also, of course, if properly
understood, indicate the levers whereby the rate of growth
can be raised. This is by no means a new enquiry. It could be
called, indeed, the revival of a classical enquiry, which until
fairly recently had been talked out or submerged. One might
suppose that any postulate about conditions of dynamic equilibrium, if it is more than a so-called 'definitional equation', implies the existence of some limiting factor or factors (the independent variables of the equation), whether or not analysis of
these factors is carried very far. But this depends, of course, on
how such equations are interpreted; and most income-expenditure equations seem to have been designed to stress the preserva-
tion of a balance as a necessary condition of development rather
than to depict one factor or group of factors as more limiting
than others (if one excepts the rather trivial statement that
growth is limited by the size of the investment-ratio and the
capital-output ratio). An attempt will be made in what follows
to examine two alternative (possibly complementary) hypo-
theses as to the investment-potential of an economy, and hence
of its growth-potential in so far as this depends upon investment
policy.

II

DISCOUNTING THE FUTURE

WHEN enunciating 'optimum conditions' for maximizing welfare, it has been customary for writers on the economics of welfare to include a condition governing the distribution of resources over time, or in other words the rate of investment. This has taken the form of postulating an equality between the rate of time preference for consumable income in the present compared to consumable income in the future and the 'rate of transformation' of present goods into future goods in production, or the marginal productivity of investment.* Thus Mr. Little states as his investment condition that: "The rate at which any given present good can be transformed into the same good, at some given future date, ought to be equal to the common marginal rate at which individuals are willing to substitute one for the other." † When a condition of this kind is given real content, it is commonly taken to mean that the government should only invest (once a state of full employment has been reached) as much as it can raise by the sale of bonds to individuals at a rate of interest that is equal to the anticipated marginal productivity of investment. ‡ The *rationale* of the suggestion is that investment should be decided by a process of 'savers' voting' on a market for loans, in the same way as the allocation of resources between different consumer goods is (or should be) determined by 'consumers' voting' on a retail market: without such a procedure there would be no 'consumers'

---

* This is not the same, of course, as the marginal productivity of the *stock* of capital, but is usually lower than this and is a function of the rate of investment.

† I. M. D. Little, *A Critique of Welfare Economics*, 2nd ed. (Oxford, 1957), p. 146.

‡ Cf. F. J. Atkinson in *Review of Economic Studies*, vol. xv, 1948, pp. 81–2.

sovereignty' regarding the allocation of resources and the flow
of consumable income over time. It is in this sense that Mr.
Little interprets the principle and it is in this sense that we
shall start discussing it.*

An initial question that arises concerns the practical meaning
to be given in this context to the "rate of transformation of
present goods into future goods", or "the marginal productivity of investment". This is quite commonly treated as being
analogous (if not identical) with the rate of profit that the investment would earn in a capitalist economy: i.e. with the future
product of investment after first deducting the values of *other*
factors of production, such as labour, employed along with the
capital goods in question. But when we are looking at the matter
from the social standpoint, why should profitability be the criterion, even if we ignore external effects? Why should not the
social return on investment be regarded as being the *total* resulting addition to national output, without any such deduction of
the values of other factors? In other words, why should it not
be indentified with the inverse of the capital : output ratio
(Domar's 'investment productivity')?

The former interpretation seems only defensible on the assumption that the supply of all other factors of production is
constant over time. In such circumstances it would no doubt be
correct to calculate only the additional product resulting from
the use of more capital with the *same* amount of labour (i.e. one
would be concerned with calculating the effect of a given degree
of 'deepening', and in the case of any particular investment
project it would be right to assess its result in terms of the
resulting net output *minus* the wage-cost of that output). But
the more usual context of investment policy is likely to be one

---

* One should perhaps explain that Mr. Little himself points out that the principle
thus interpreted depends on "making a number of most unrealistic assumptions",
and goes on to show that an alternative interpretation is possible, whereby it is not
individual time-preferences but "the government's relative scheduled values for
future products over present products" that are the basis of the investment condition (*ibid.*, pp. 149, 150). This is the interpretation given by Professor Bergson
who, in applying to capital goods the condition that "the marginal productivity of
each factor must be the same in every industry", supposes (a) that capital goods
are valued at the "discounted value" of their future "marginal value productivity
in the consumers' goods industries", (b) that the appropriate rate of discount is the
rate at which the Government Planning Board "discounts future in comparison
with present income", leaving open the question of how the Board arrives at this
discount (*A Survey of Contemporary Economics*, I, ed. Howard S. Ellis, 1948, p. 421).

in which the supply of labour in employment is changing, either because of population increase or because there is a reserve of labour to be drawn into employment *pari passu* with the progress of investment.* That part of the growth of the national income which provides wage-goods for the additionally employed seems to be as deserving of inclusion in the reckoning as that part which is surplus to the wages of the additionally employed; since from the community's point of view the possession of additional equipment that will enable one at future dates to afford more employment to labour is, surely, part of the benefit of investment. As Dr. A. K. Sen has put it in replying to Professor Tinbergen: "For the purpose of the choice of *social* optimum rate of saving it is the capital coefficient, and not the capital-interest ratio, which is relevant." † If the rate of investment were to be settled (as *inter alia* Mr. F. J. Atkinson proposed) by the verdict of a government bond market, the return offered to bondholders would need to be equal to this social investment-coefficient: a necessity which does not seem to have been contemplated by the sponsors of such proposals, and one likely to have some awkward practical consequences.

Another difficulty about this 'individualist' proposal is that it presupposes that the individual can know what the income of himself, his children and their children will be at future dates; since without such knowledge there can be no rational basis for his time-preference. This seems to be not merely a highly unrealistic assumption (as Mr. Little admits that it is), but one involving circular reasoning, since it postulates that total investment is arrived at by aggregating the savings-decisions of individuals who, acting as independent units, base these decisions on certain assumptions about future national income (and its distribution) when the future trend of the national income will depend upon the size of this investment total (in the present and in future years). This is completely analogous with the case we considered in Chapter I of investment decisions taken atomistically by individual *entrepreneurs*. Each individual *could* only act

---

* At first sight this case might seem to be covered by the qualification, "once a state of full employment has been reached", in the above-cited investment-condition. But this is only partly so, since the "state of full employment" there mentioned refers to the condition prevailing at the time that the investment is first made and *not* to the possibility of a surplus of labour at future dates when the capital equipment in question is in use.   † *Economic Journal*, Dec. 1957, p. 747.

objectively on the basis of knowledge of all relevant factors if decision were in some sense a collective one and *not* a sum of independent individual decisions; in which case they would collectively act quite differently from the way they will act severally. At any rate, it is obvious that relevant criteria cannot be derived from any market data (the conditions for a futures market just do not exist).*

But there is a more fundamental objection than either of these to an individualist criterion of this kind: namely, that individuals' choices over time are notoriously irrational, perhaps not invariably but at any rate quite commonly; so much so that economists have come to regard it as a 'natural' element forming part of the data in the problem of interest and of investment. This, however, is no good reason why the State, *qua* custodian of future generations as well as the present, should adopt this irrationality as its own. The irrationality consists in discounting the future *solely* because of the passage of time (i.e. apart from differences in income over time or uncertainty regarding it). If one is likely to be the same person five years hence, and to have roughly the same real income, the gift of a certain enjoyment, whether it be a crate of champagne or a visit to the Sistine Chapel, will add the same amount to the pleasures of a lifetime whether it is promised in five years' time or today. If one places a premium on having it today, this can only be a sign of weakness of will or of temperament—a defect of the 'telescopic faculty' (as Pigou so aptly put it). In our rational moments we surely would not want our planners to imitate this defect. Clearly, for planning purposes "we are interested in tomorrow's satisfaction as such, not in today's assessment of tomorrow's satisfaction".† This is a matter that has been so much discussed that I think we need only affirm with Ramsey that to "discount later enjoyments in comparison with earlier ones" is "a practice which is ethically indefensible and arises merely from the weakness of the imagination".‡ We cannot derive any investment-

* Cf. J. de V. Graaf: "No one household has any way of knowing what other households intend to do. The market does not provide it with the information it requires to make a rational decision. . . . The ordinary mechanism of the market cannot handle it." (*Theoretical Welfare Economics* (Cambridge, 1957), p. 103.)

† A. K. Sen, *loc. cit.*, p. 746.

‡ F. P. Ramsey, 'A Mathematical Theory of Saving', in *Economic Journal*, Dec., 1928, p. 543. Cf. also Mr. Harrod's reference to "pure time preference" as "a polite expression for rapacity and the conquest of reason by passion" (*op. cit.*, p. 40).

criterion from individual savings-decisions, whether registered on a market or in some other way.

Can we, however, find a criterion that would correspond to the formal condition that we have quoted without resting on individual attitudes and behaviour? If so, this could serve as an *a priori* principle from which planners would be able to derive their own weighting of future benefit and present cost. To say that from a social standpoint there should be no time discount, so far as discount for time *per se* is concerned, is not to say that a socialist state should attach equal weight to an increment of social income irrespective of the date at which it accrues. To do so unconditionally would, of course, lead to the situation where one was always ready to starve oneself in the present so long as there was any annual benefit however small to be derived from adding to the community's stock of capital (as Professor Robertson has said, even a one per cent return when multiplied by infinity is greater than 100*—and the same is true of a hundredth of one per cent return). If income in the future (at least, if this is income per head) is likely to be greater than it is today, it is quite reasonable to attach smaller weight to a given increment in the future than to the same increment today (and conversely if income in the future is likely to be smaller). If growth is occurring at all, total income (though not necessarily *per capita*) *must* be rising over time; and if it were not occurring one would not be discussing the situation in terms of dynamic theory. At first sight, therefore, it might seem easy enough to deduce an investment rule from the so-called 'law of diminishing utility' that the additional utility or welfare to be derived from the enjoyment of a given (small) addition to income falls as that income grows larger. One could derive it, for example, from the famous Ramsey-theorem, which on the assumption that this rate of fall is constant and that there exists a finite "maximum attainable rate of enjoyment" (Bliss) derives the optimum rate of investment directly from the rate of fall of marginal utility by an elegantly simple formula (if the elasticity of the curve expressing the fall of utility with rising

* Sir Dennis Robertson, *Lectures on Economic Principles*, vol. ii (London, 1958), p. 89; cf. J. Tinbergen, 'The Optimum Rate of Saving', in *Economic Journal*, Dec. 1956, p. 609.

income is η, then η will be the proportion of income to be invested).*

Unfortunately on examination the apparent simplicity of this approach proves to be deceptive. An initial difficulty I shall mention only to dismiss it as not one of fundamental moment (though others might not agree): Is it right to interpret such a principle in terms of change in *per capita* income—or is this simply another instance of the individualist fallacy? And what of the case where growth only just suffices to keep pace with population increase and there is no rise in *per capita* income: how is this to be fitted into our calculus? The 'law of diminishing utility' was never intended to refer to anything but changes in *individual* incomes. At any rate, what plausibility it can claim, surely, vanishes as soon as one applies it to total income irrespective of the number of individuals enjoying it.

To take this second question first: the case of growth with constant *per capita* income seems to be less difficult than might at first sight appear, even if it does involve us in an issue which nineteenth-century utilitarians found great difficulty in resolving. In this case one could, I think, reasonably hold that provision for employing the expected increase of population at the same standard of consumption as the present should be given priority over provision for raising the standard of those already in employment. This would then stand as a *minimum* requirement; and it would follow that if current investment were less than sufficient to do this, investment should be raised at the expense of reducing present consumption, until provision was enough to maintain the future at the same standard as the consumption standard of today. Investment above this minimum requirement, having the effect not merely of stabilizing but of raising the standard of living over time, could then be left to be determined by the diminishing-utility rule. It is an evident corollary (in the spirit of *The Economics of Welfare*) that, with national income at all future dates given, and with a given rate of population increase, it is preferable that this income at any of these dates should be evenly divided over the whole popula-

---

* Cf. Ramsey, *loc. cit.*; also Sir Dennis Robertson, *op. cit.*, p. 90. Those who will not accept the 'law of diminishing utility' because they 'deny' the possibility of interpersonal comparisons seem to be precluded from saying anything about distribution over time, since it is surely much more difficult to make interpersonal comparisons between *generations* than between contemporary individuals.

tion than that some should have a sufficiency or more and the residue lack a means of livelihood. But it should be noted that this corollary (which works in favour of maximizing employment as a prior objective) does not follow if the national income at future dates is not independent of the choice one is making; as in the case we shall consider later where the alternative is between an investment policy that increases employment at the earliest possible date but at the expense of future growth and a policy that yields a lower level of employment (and with it of aggregate consumption) in the near future, but with the promise of a more rapid expansion subsequently. If the principle of diminishing utility can yield any guiding rule in such a case (e.g. by the integration of utilities over time), this will not be a simple one.

But the more fundamental difficulty, and the one that seems to be decisive, is the practical difficulty of giving any real meaning to the marginal utility of income to a representative individual of the community at different income-levels, at any rate when those different incomes accrue at different dates, separated by substantial intervals of time. This is not simply a difficulty of practical verification. If it were no more than this, some approximate indicators at least of the relationship might be derived from the behaviour (e.g. in response to taxation or wage-changes) of various income-groups; and it is conceivable at any rate that tests could be devised to ascertain the income-elasticity of demand for consumption goods in general, as well as for particular goods. It is the difficulty of giving any meaning to the relationship at all, at any rate any relevant meaning that would make it capable of operational use. To be usable as an investment-criterion it must evidently be capable of application *ex ante*. It is useless as a simple record *ex post* of what has occurred when income has changed in the past—useless without some rational ground for extrapolating past trends into the future. But a changing income-level of a whole community is part of a process of economic development into which historical change essentially enters, such that man himself is altered in the process and not only the supply of things which cater for his scale of wants. Economic development consists as much of multiplying products and varying the assortment as in augmenting the supply of an existing catalogue or menu of products; and in this

innovating process the causal influence of new products upon
new wants is at least as powerful as the converse. It could, indeed, be plausibly argued that this is a situation to which the
notion of producers' sovereignty, not consumers' sovereignty,
essentially applies. Enough at any rate has been talked in recent
years about the importance of conventional elements in wants,
in the guise of Duesenberry's demonstration-effects and other
Veblenesque phenomena, to make further elaboration of the
point otiose.* Such elements seem to be sufficient to render
nugatory the search for any calculable stable relation between
consumable income and utility, and probably to make the
very notion of such a relationship worthless.

The problem nonetheless remains of attaching *some* discount
to additional income at future dates as a limit upon any investment programme. If it were merely a matter of fixing a ceiling
to investment, one might say that, in the absence of an economic
criterion, the very notion of comparing income at different
points of time was a superfluous piece of analytical machinery,
and that one would do better simply to fix a politically feasible
ceiling and not to seek justification for it by spurious appeals to
a time-discount. However, it is not enough merely to fix an
overall investment total. One has also to make particular investment projects consistent with it— consistent, not merely in the
sense that they are made to add up to the required total (this
could presumably be achieved by a process of trial and error,
punctuated by appropriate prunings), but in the sense that
every particular investment project fulfils at least a minimum
requirement as regards the relation between its promised results
and what it costs. Ideally the setting of the correct minimum
requirement should itself enable the cost of all the separate
projects to add up to the required total; so that for practical
purposes one could either proceed by setting the minimum
requirement for projects and let the result determine aggregate
investment, or else fix the overall total and then bring the minimum requirement into corresponding relation with it, the latter

---

* Cf. J. S. Duesenberry's remark that "the preference system in existence at one
moment is the consequence of actual purchases in the past. We cannot say that our
problem is to find how the system adapts to the data if the data are changing with
the adaptation." Elsewhere he says: "The mechanism which connects consumption decisions is not that of rational planning but of learning and habit formation."
(*Income, Saving and the Theory of Consumer Behaviour* (Harvard, 1949), pp. 14, 24.)

then serving simply as a rationing-device in allocating the investment fund. But the chief *raison d'être* of the minimum requirement is to make the most effective use of the investible resources available, and to make the technical forms in which these resources are embodied in various industries consistent with one another by imposing a uniform criterion.

This aspect of the investment problem has appeared in the discussion among Soviet economists and planners in the form of calculating the 'economic effectiveness of investment'; and the prominent part this discussion has played over a number of years, both among those at the industrial or departmental level concerned with the concrete detail of investment projects (especially in transport and electrical power generation) and at the national level (e.g. in Gosplan and in institutes of the Academy of Sciences) can be taken as a witness to the important place this problem occupies in the practice of a planned economy. It has been, apparently, a common practice to employ a minimum coefficient as a criterion of choice between alternative technical variants, in two forms (one being simply the inverse of the other) referred to respectively as a coefficient of effectiveness and a period of recoupment, and customarily symbolized by the letters Э and O. These, when represented as the difference between two alternative projects (differing both in their initial investment cost and in their subsequent result in terms of productivity), are defined as follows:

$$\Theta = \frac{C_1 - C_2}{K_2 - K_1}$$

$$O = \frac{K_2 - K_1}{C_1 - C_2}$$

where C_1 and C_2 stand for the operational cost, or prime cost,[*] of a given annual output under the two methods when these are in use, and K_1 and K_2 for the initial construction costs of the two capital projects under comparison.[†] It will be clear that such

---

[*] Including amortization allowance.

[†] See *Voprosi Ekonomiki*, 1954, no. 3, p. 109. Professor T. S. Khachaturov in his book *Osnovy Ekonomiki Zheleznodorozhnogo Transporta* (Economic Principles of Railway Transport), Moscow, 1946, pt. i, chap. iii, writes as follows of the recoupment period: "Thus, let the capital investment for building an electrified railway be

coefficients can also be used in the comparison of two investment projects of different durabilities or of the investment of an
initial sum now (e.g. in a double-track railway) and a larger
total investment with only half of it required now (in a single
track only) and the other half at some later date (this second
alternative having the advantage of postponing part of the investment to a date when resources are more plentiful, though
with the disadvantage of a higher total expenditure). If ϑ is
taken as some standard coefficient of effectiveness, then investments at future dates can be equated to present values for
purpose of comparison by multiplying them by $1/(1 + \vartheta)^t$.*

However, these coefficients, by reason of their empirical
origin, have been apt to differ in different industries (e.g. an
effectiveness coefficient of 6 per cent being employed in the
projecting of hydro-electric stations and of 10 per cent in the
case of railways), † and no uniform coefficient has been imposed.
Rather incomprehensibly, this diversity of practice even found
some defenders. An interim report on the discussion of these
methods (arising out of a conference organized jointly by the
Department of Economics and Law of the Academy of Sciences
and the journal *Voprosi Ekonomiki* in 1954) pronounced in favour
of such methods of calculation in principle and of their general
use as indices in choosing between investment alternatives within a given economic sector; rejecting the view of those (such as
Mstislavsky) who had criticized such indices as inadmissible and
worthless. Not surprisingly they failed to agree on any principle

90 million roubles and for the same railway to operate with steam-traction 70 million roubles, while the operating expenses per year are 2.5 million and 5 million
roubles respectively. After a period t, equal to 8 years, the economy in operating
expenses will match the extra outlay required for the electrified line. . . . The value
obtained for t is to be compared with a maximum period t_o, established in advance,
within which any extra investment outlay must, as a rule, be recouped through
savings in operating expenses. If the period t is longer than t_o, i.e. if it is necessary
to wait too long for the more expensive variant to pay for itself, then obviously
preference must be given to the cheaper alternative. If the period t is shorter than
t_o, the expensive alternative will be the more profitable." Speaking of the coefficient of effectiveness, he says that this "as a method of calculation has been
found absolutely essential in planning practice, because without it no calculations
for comparing investment alternatives could be made. Methods of comparing
capital outlays and operating expenses put forward by project-makers have been
prompted by life itself, and have to some extent been diffused in practical work."
(*cit*. Holland Hunter in *Review of Economics and Statistics*, Feb. 1949, p. 55.)

* *Voprosi Ekonomiki*, 1954, no. 3, pp. 111–12; T. S. Khachaturov, *op. cit*., pp.
107–8.   † *Voprosi Ekonomiki*, 1954, no. 3, p. 110.

for deriving a uniform coefficient for the economy as a whole; and no reference was apparently made to the view, expressed by Professor Khachaturov and adopted in the main by a conference convened by the Railway Research Institute some years before,* that the appropriate coefficient would tend to fall in the course of Socialist construction as a result of the growth in the stock of capital. It was agreed however that the whole topic was deserving of further discussion and study; and there is at the time of writing a special Scientific Council concerned with this question in the Department of Economics, Philosophy and Law of the Academy. †

This type of ratio, connecting investment cost with future output (or economies in the cost of output), will be affected, of course, by any change in the relative prices of capital goods and the particular output in question (or alternatively of the main constituents of the cost of this output, e.g. wages); and expressed as it usually must be in terms of price, the significance of such a ratio can be said to be vitiated by any 'arbitrary' element in the structure of relative prices (unless this 'arbitrary' influence affects all alternatives under comparison in a similar way, and in similar degree, and so does not affect the comparison of them in terms of greater or less). As is well known, there is in the U.S.S.R. a substantial difference between the price-levels of the consumer goods sector and the capital goods sector, products of the former being subject to turnover tax and products of the latter, save in some special cases, being exempt. It would be possible, of course, in both cases to use cost-prices, rather than actual sales-prices, as a basis for calculating investment ratios;

* Reported in *Tekhnika Zheleznykh Dorog*, 1947, no. 5 (for this reference the writer is indebted to Mr. Holland Hunter).

† According to a recent article, "what is essentially new in the proposed research work [of this Scientific Council] is the study of the actual effectiveness of capital investments carried out in the past, and also the utilization of the results of this study as the basis for working out the theory of this problem", the target-date for completing this work being 1960 (V. Petrov in *Voprosi Ekonomiki*, 1958, no. 1, pp. 111–12). In June 1958 an all-Union scientific-technical conference was held in Moscow on this subject; a lengthy report of the conference, together with summary 'recommendations' of it, being published in *Voprosi Ekonomiki*, 1958, no. 9, pp. 119–62. It may be of some interest to note that in one of the two main reports to the conference (the other was by Professor Khachaturov) Academician Strumilin identified Э (the coefficient of effectiveness) with $\Delta\pi/\Delta\varphi$ where $\Delta\pi$ represents the rise of production, "in natural units or in constant prices", and $\Delta\varphi$ additional capital funds (pp. 122–3).

and if the investment-cost of capital goods is being compared
with savings in prime cost or operating costs in various lines of
production, this is in effect what is being done. In this case the
result could be acquitted, it would seem, of arbitrary valuation.
It is, however, this kind of defect that critics of these ratios
chiefly have in mind, apparently Strumilin in particular. Strumilin, accordingly (in his now well-known but somewhat baff-
ling article of 1946)* sought to find a basis for an investment
criterion in the rate of growth of labour productivity over time.
The *rationale* of this suggestion seems to be that because a given
income will be more easily obtainable (in the sense of involving
less cost in social labour) at future dates, it should be accorded
a lower weight in planning calculations than present income.
If the suggestion is regarded as simply affording a theoretical
ground for the existence of some time-discount in investment
decisions, there is a good deal to be said in its favour. In terms
consistent with the labour theory of value it seizes upon a crucial
aspect of the process of development which is manifestly significant for investment policy. One could say, indeed, that in stressing the rising productivity of human effort it concentrates upon
the obverse side of the same phenomenon as has been the con-
cern of those who have focused attention upon rising income per
head. In attempting, however, to make the rate of increase of
labour productivity the basis for fixing what the discount-
coefficient shall be, it seems to be no more surely grounded than
the other attempts we have mentioned.† In one respect it can
be said to be less plausible than the others, since the problem
we are discussing is essentially one connected with a change in
products regarded as use-values, not as exchange-values, and
the significance of changing productivity, in the context in

* S. G. Strumilin, 'The Time-factor in Capital Investment Projects', in *Izvestia
Akademii Nauk S.S.S.R.*, Economics and Law Series, 1946, no. 3; republished in
Eng. trans. in *International Economic Papers*, no. 1.

† What concretely Strumilin seems to be suggesting is that the minimum requirement for an investment should be that it is capable of increasing net output in
value-terms (i.e. allowing for the fall of values generally over its lifetime) by an
amount equal to the difference between the value of the initial investment and its
replacement-value at the end of its life; this latter difference measuring the increase
of labour-productivity over the period in question. Alternatively, $\Sigma V^{1-n} = I - R$,
where V stands for the value of the additional output, I for the original value of
the investment and R for its replacement value at the end of its life. (Cf. N. Kaplan,
'Investment Alternatives in Soviet Economic Theory', in *Journal of Political
Economy*, April 1952, p. 139.)

which Strumilin is dealing with it, is for value in the second of
the two classical senses and not in the first. Near the beginning
of his article, indeed, he recognizes the importance of the use-
value aspect, but seems to suggest that to measure it and to
measure the decline in labour-value comes to the same thing.
He writes: "In a planned socialist economy production is
undertaken for the sake of *use* (consumption) and additional
investments of past labour may be justified by the creation—
with the same quantity of living labour—of an additional
quantity of consumption goods, or alternatively by a reduction
in the quantity of labour required to maintain the same scale of
production of consumption goods." And again: "In our country we are interested not so much in the degree and the rate of
accumulation as in its productive effect in physical units of output. But this effect is linked with the loss in the value of the
products of past labour."* To say, however, that two things are
linked is not to say that the movement of one is a significant
index of the movement of the other; and there is no reason to
suppose that the fall in value is a significant measure of the
increase in use-values, even if a fall in the human cost of maintaining a certain level of output is an element in the total
reckoning: there is even some reason for treating it as an un-
satisfactory measure.

The conclusion seems to be that the search for an investment
criterion along the lines we have indicated has yielded a negligible harvest for the economic planner. Once the overall rate
of investment has been decided upon, an appropriate minimum
ratio of effectiveness or rate of return can be arrived at, which
if uniformly applied would make the investment projects chosen
add up to the decided total. But this can only be arrived at by
trial and error, and cannot be independently reached and used
to determine what the rate of investment itself shall be. It may
be said that clarity of thought in at least defining the nature of
the problem has been reached by an approach along such lines,
even if real content in a quantitative mould cannot be introduced into this definition. It may also be claimed that we can
be sure, at any rate, that *some* discount on time is better than
none. However, since this is equivalent to saying that one should
not invest the whole national income, which is a conclusion that

* *International Economic Papers*, no. 1, pp. 161, 171.

any planner could reach by quite unsophisticated common sense, this is not a great claim for a theory of time-discount to make.

As we said towards the end of the previous chapter, in any given situation the range of choice regarding the rate of investment is always much narrower than the type of analysis we have discussed in this section implies. At any rate it is much narrower so far as *raising* it at will is concerned: one could always lower it presumably if one did not mind leaving actual or potential resources unutilized; although it would not follow that if one did so this would raise the consumable income of the present. Any search for a criterion of an optimum policy implies the kind of analysis that deals in terms of the long long-period when all eggs can be unscrambled and constants converted into variables; and this serves to explain the air of unreality that such an approach has for many readers. In so far as planning can reach forward into such a long-period, this kind of approach, as we have said, would not be pointless if it yielded any fruit. As it is, an economist may be better employed more modestly, for the time being at least, in asking more short-period questions about the determinants of the investment-decision in particular situations; and then seeing whether this can get him any further in terms of a series of generations of new particular situations (each with its special constraints) out of those that have gone before. In this way it is possible that he may be able to say something useful about the internal relations of the process of growth.

III

CHOICE OF TECHNIQUE IN THE
CONSUMER GOODS SECTOR:
A SIMPLE MODEL

WE shall in this chapter and the two following it try to work out the implications for growth of two alternative assumptions about what is the crucial investment determinant; after which we can see whether the resulting models can be related to one another and possibly combined.

Let us take first the case where the basic determinant of how much an economy can devote to real investment at any given time is the surplus of consumer goods production over what is consumed by the producers of these goods themselves. This simple notion has no attraction of novelty: it is indeed a very classical assumption, which runs through the work of the early economists, lurked somewhat obscurely behind the wages-fund controversy and subsequently appeared in certain well-known versions of capital theory in the guise of a 'subsistence fund'. It can lay some claim to realism in that it seems to correspond to the actual lineaments of the economic problem in many underdeveloped countries; although this correspondence is clouded a little by the fact that it is there the size of the actually *marketed* surplus of a peasant agriculture that forms, apparently, the bottle-neck from which all development plans for the industrial sector have to build (and what is marketed may be largely influenced by relative prices, tax policy, etc.). Without an expansion of this marketed portion of agricultural output no attempt to expand industrial employment (and with it urban food consumption) or (since export-goods as well as wage-goods come from agriculture) to increase the import of industrial equipment can meet with any ultimate success. Nor will a rise in total agricultural output, even if it is a rise in output per head, necessarily make any contribution to the problem, since it may be absorbed in higher consumption by the peasant producers themselves—a fact that was very much in the forefront of discussion and policy-making in the U.S.S.R. in the '20s. In such circumstances a price-policy, however favourable to agriculture, may not suffice to attract a larger flow of village products on to the urban market, since the peasant may be content to take out the benefit of improved terms of trade in getting more industrial products for the *same* total quantity of agricultural exports as formerly (possibly even for less). And if industrial products are scarce, owing to the weak development of industry and restricted import-possibilities, even such a price-policy may be precluded. A tax policy, however, if suitably devised, may succeed (as in Japan) in raising the marketed surplus both relatively and absolutely.

To give any precision to the notion of a surplus in the consumer goods sector, one must postulate a certain 'necessary' level of wages, introducing into the definition of 'necessary' as many social and conventional, or even 'political', elements as one wishes. In other words, while this wage is to be treated as an essential minimum, it need not be a purely physical-subsistence wage, as the 'subsistence wage' of the classical economists is commonly (but not necessarily correctly) represented as being. In what follows we shall assume for simplicity that this wage is constant (also uniform between different economic sectors). But one could alternatively treat it as rising over time, either as a function of time or of rising productivity;* thereby in effect introducing into one's assumption about wage-policy any welfare premiss about changing consumption-standards over time (or about the proportions of income to be respectively consumed and 'saved').

A condition for any growth at all is the existence of such a surplus, in order to supply the consumption (at the necessary

---

* Provided that it does not rise in the same (or greater) proportion as productivity. To treat it, however, as rising with productivity would be to qualify its 'necessary' character to the point of modifying some of the corollaries to be discussed below.

wage) of workers employed in the sector of industry producing capital goods, which we may call for short the investment sector. If capital goods have to be replaced at intervals, then of course a certain minimum size of the investment sector is necessary for this purpose (and a corresponding part of the surplus of consumer goods is not a pure surplus but a depreciation or amortisation cost); and it is only any output of capital goods above this replacement level that qualifies as net investment and constitutes the growth-potential of the system. We can get round the awkwardness introduced into our analysis by this consideration if we assume—at the cost of ignoring the replacement problem—that capital goods once created last for ever, provided that they are currently maintained; maintenance of capital goods employed in the consumer goods sector being done by the workers in that sector, and time spent on such maintenance work being included in the wage-cost of output and allowed for in calculating the average workers' productivity. We can then treat the *whole* of the labour-force in the investment sector as contributing to an increase in the stock of capital equipment; and if there is any investment sector at all some growth is occurring.

If we were to assume the labour force to be of a constant size, without any reserve or prospect of natural increase, the investment sector (measured in terms of employment) could only grow by drawing labour away from the other sector, and doing so without any loss of surplus in that sector. This would impose the necessity of progressively altering the capital goods turned out by the investment sector in a labour-saving direction; and this would in turn involve the scrapping of capital goods of obsolete types in order to release labour from operating them, so that part of the output of the investment sector would always, in effect, be replacing obsolete capital equipment instead of contributing to growth.* In these circumstances the choice of technical form of investment (or *type* of capital goods turned out) would be dictated jointly by the requirements of the labour situation and the prospective growth-rate; and it is scarcely

---

* It would, of course, be contributing to growth of output to the extent of the *difference* between labour productivity with the equipment currently being turned out and labour productivity with the equipment it replaces, but by no more than this.

conceivable that a *declining* growth-rate of national output could
be avoided, unless technical invention was proceeding at a
requisite pace. We shall not, however, at the outset make this
restrictive assumption about the labour force; but shall wait to
introduce it as a special case later on. We shall start by assuming
what corresponds pretty closely to the situation in most underdeveloped economies: that there is a large reserve of labour,
either unemployed or employed at a very low level of productivity or else belonging to a purely subsistence economy on the
periphery of the economic system that we are considering.*
We do not need to assume, however, that the wage in industry
is equal to either the standard of life of this reserve or the low-
level productivity of those attached to the peripheral subsistence
economy. It would indeed be unrealistic to do so. Industrial
work has its own subsistence standards, apart from social and
trade union requirements; and a marked feature, again, of
underdeveloped countries, even where trade unions are weak,
is the substantial differential existing between industrial wages
and the rural income level, which is more than can be explained
simply by immobility. There are, indeed, those who have maintained that it is the (low or zero) productivity of labour in these
marginal occupations of the 'disguised unemployed' that should
be treated from the social point of view as the 'cost of labour'.
But this is a questionable contention, save as a way of postulating that maximizing employment immediately should be the
objective of economic policy; and it has little bearing on the
problem that we are discussing here, which concerns surplus as
an investment determinant, to the size of which the actual wage
that must be paid, and not any notional wage, can alone be
relevant.

Since in the circumstances we have described the potential
rate of investment (measured in terms of labour employed in
the investment sector) † is fixed by the size of the existing surplus

* One could alternatively assume that the natural rate of increase of the population is greater than the maximum probable growth-rate of the economy. As regards
the unemployed and unproductively employed, one can assume that they are
living on their relatives or alternatively by mendicancy or petty theft. On this kind
of assumption, which is a common one nowadays in discussions of under-developed
countries, see Nurkse on 'disguised unemployment', *op. cit.*, pp. 32–6, where he
states that "the marginal productivity of labour over a wide range is zero".

† At any given level of labour-productivity in this sector the rate of investment
measured in terms of output is similarly fixed.

in the consumer goods sector, the only degree of freedom open to investment policy is the choice of the technical form of the investment (or the type of capital good to produce for eventual use by the consumer goods sector).

In the light of what the Harrod-Domar type of equation tells us, it might seem to follow that even this degree of freedom does not really exist, at any rate if an increase in the growth-rate is held to be a desirable objective. If we take the simple Harrodian $GC = s$, and assume that s is given* (as we have in effect done by postulating a given rate of surplus in the consumer goods sector), there would appear to be only one technical choice consistent with maximizing G: namely, to choose the form of investment with the lowest capital-output ratio, C. The analogous Domar equation of the growth-rate with the product of the savings-ratio and the coefficient of investment productivity could be taken to yield the same corollary—that with the savings-ratio given, the coefficient of investment productivity (the inverse of the investment-output ratio) should be made as high as possible.

Such a corollary has, indeed, found currency in economic literature about underdeveloped countries, and has even come to be treated as axiomatic. It has often been identified with what one may call the theory of factor-proportions: that the choice of technique should depend upon the existing factor-endowment (in the sense of the relative supplies of different factors) in a country at any particular stage of development. This identification is implicit, for example, in the following passage from a United Nations Report:†

---

*G stands for the growth-rate, C for the capital-output ratio and s for the savings-ratio. Bringing in income explicitly and using Y for income, I for total investment and similarly S for total savings, this can be translated into:

$$\frac{\Delta Y}{Y} \cdot \frac{I}{\Delta Y} = \frac{S}{Y}$$

† *Processes and Problems of Industrialization in Under-Developed Countries* (United Nations, 1955), p. 48. Cf. also R. Nurkse, *op. cit.*, p. 45; Dr. H. W. Singer in *Formulation and Economic Appraisal of Development Projects* (U.N., 1951), pp. 31, 34; Norman S. Buchanan and Howard S. Ellis, *Approaches to Economic Development* (New York, 1955), p. 275: "A general commonsense presumption exists for using the scarce and expensive factor of capital sparingly relatively to labour", also pp. 276–7; G. M. Meier and R. E. Baldwin, *Economic Development: Theory, History, Policy* (New York, 1957), p. 349: "Since in the poor country the social price of labour is likely to be low or even zero compared with the price of capital, a relatively high ratio of labour to capital will be favoured."

"By and large the most suitable technologies are likely to be those which yield the maximum social return per unit of capital, reckoning labour at its social cost rather than market cost. In many instances this means that the answer probably lies in the direction of choosing the simplest of alternative techniques . . . the smallest type of plant consistent with technical efficiency, the technology that makes the best use of the most plentiful factors of production. Multi-storied factories are usually inappropriate in areas where land is abundant; wheelbarrows may be more suitable than conveyor-belts where capital is scarce and the marginal productivity of labour in traditional occupations is near zero."

Already the Indian Five Year Plan in its Draft Outline* had taken it for granted that "in a country in which labour is plentiful relatively to capital, preference must be given . . . to labour-intensive rather than capital-intensive techniques". Actually the two theories (that the minimum investment-output ratio should be chosen in the interests of growth and that technique should be adapted to the prevailing factor-proportions) need to be differentiated, since it is only in a particular situation and on special assumptions† that they yield identical criteria; and these are not the assumptions of our present model.

Is it correct to suppose that such a corollary is contained in the Harrod or Domar equation? It is a commonplace that equations are only made to yield causal statements by importing additional postulates about the variables, in particular how far any of them can be treated as independent variables. Indeed, Mr. Harrod was himself at pains to emphasize that his equation

* Government of India Planning Commission (July, 1951), p. 19.

† These assumptions are that relative factor prices are proportional to the relative marginal productivities of factors when all factors are fully employed in circumstances that permit of the full range (if need be) of technically-feasible factor-substitution being explored. The pattern of factor prices will then influence the pattern of comparative costs of different forms of investment, so that those forms of investment which use relatively much of the plentiful factors and equivalently economize on the scarce factors are the cheapest. On the further assumption that the productivity of labour is independent of its price, this productivity can be treated as varying solely with the factor combination: e.g. the capital-to-labour ratio. If we take labour to be the plentiful factor and capital the scarce, then, provided that the productivity of labour varies less than proportionately with variation in the ratio of capital to labour (the usual assumption implicit in a factor-substitution curve, or isoquant), the ratio of output to capital will rise as technical-substitution proceeds in a more labour-using direction until this ratio (of output to capital) is maximized as wages approach zero (or when full employment is reached—whichever happens sooner).

referring to a 'warranted rate of growth' was no more than a truism.

When one is dealing with a capitalist economy one may or may not be justified in treating the capital-output ratio and the savings ratio as independent of each other. There is some plausibility at least in supposing that they are not at all closely related, seeing that savings are the product of a multitude of individual decisions about the disposal of individual incomes, and there is some empirical evidence for doubting whether, in the long run at least, the proportion of these incomes that is saved is markedly affected by changes in average income (as distinct from its distribution). But this plausibility vanishes when one is referring to a socialist economy, since there it is clear that any change in productivity, in face of a given level of real wages, must affect directly or indirectly the resources available to the State for investment. In the two-sector model we have outlined it is clear that for every level of productivity in the consumer goods sector there will be a different level of surplus, and hence a different investment-potential. According as the current investment-potential is used to produce capital goods of different types, it will be introducing different levels of productivity into the consumer goods sector (when these capital goods are installed and in operation) and hence different rates of surplus per unit of labour employed there. These different types of capital goods will also entail different costs to produce; and one could arrange the alternatives in a list or series that showed on the one hand rising costs and on the other hand rising productivities when in use.* Once we allow for the effect of raising the productivity upon the surplus-ratio, and hence upon future investment-potential, it will no longer follow that the choice of the one that shows the lowest ratio of cost to productivity is alone consistent with maximum growth.

To revert to our model: the notation that we have used on two previous occasions may as well serve to assist in concise

* It will not, of course, follow that in listing all the possible alternatives a higher cost will always be associated with higher productivity; but those that show higher cost without any higher productivity than another in the list will not be worth including, and will accordingly be rejected from the final list of alternatives deserving consideration. In the final choice all alternatives which show the same ratio of cost to productivity will be identical, and will be grouped as one; so that essentially the order of our list is an order of cost-to-productivity ratios.

exposition. If we write L for the labour-force (measured in man-hours or man-years), p for its productivity measured in product-units, with suffixes i and c to indicate the investment sector and the consumer goods sector respectively, and w for the level of wages (which is uniform in the two sectors and may be treated as measured over the same unit-period of time as productivities are measured), then our condition governing investment can be represented as:

$$L_i \cdot w = L_c \, (p_c - w)$$

$$\text{or} \quad L_i = \frac{L_c \, (p_c - w)}{w}$$

If we write, s for $(p_c - w)$, we can simplify the condition to:

$$L_i = \frac{L_c s}{w}.$$

While this condition gives us a relationship between the two sectors in terms of employment (namely, $L_i/L_c = s/w$), it does not, of course, suffice to determine the absolute size of L_i at any one time, or total employment. To do this, one has to introduce some assumption about L_c, such as that L_c is determined by the existing stock of capital equipment in that sector, from which it will follow that L_c will grow at a rate that is governed by the growth of this capital stock, and hence by the rate of investment measured in terms of the output of the investment sector ($= L_i p_i$).

For simplicity let us assume that capital equipment in the c-sector is homogeneous,* which has the convenience of enabling it to be measured in product-units; further, that the 'technical coefficient' relating capital equipment to labour when this equipment is in operation is a simple one-one relation (for example, if we think of these capital goods as tractors, then each tractor irrespective of type requires one tractor-driver).† We then have a second relationship of the form:

---

* This assumption (and the consequence of relaxing it) is further considered in a Note to this Chapter (below, p. 104 *seq.*).

† It should, perhaps, be made clear that this assumption is not equivalent to one of 'fixed coefficients' when speaking of factor-proportions (in the usual sense). But in our model change in coefficients takes exclusively the form of a change in *type* of capital equipment.

$$\frac{dL_c}{dt} = L_i p_i$$

Assuming p_i, p_c and w to be given, and L_c to have had a certain value at some initial date, these two relations provide us from their interaction with a simple growth-model; with

$$\frac{dL_i}{dt} \cdot \frac{1}{L_i} \text{ (or alternatively } \frac{dL_c}{dt} \cdot \frac{1}{L_c})$$

as the measure of proportional growth. One result of this mode of presentation is to focus attention upon the p's as factors in the growth-rate—factors which do not appear explicitly in income-expenditure balances of the Harrod-Domar type.

As soon as we introduce the possibility of alternative types of capital good, each yielding a different p_c,* it becomes clear that to choose the type with the higher value of p_c will tend, *ceteris paribus*, to raise the growth-rate by raising s/w. Since, however, a higher p_c can usually be purchased only at the expense of a higher cost in labour of producing the capital good in question, this will be true only up to a certain point. In our notation this higher cost will be represented by a *lower* p_i (cost per unit being $1/p_i$); so that beyond a certain point the fall in p_i and hence in dL_c/dt will offset the rise of $(p_c - w)/w$ or s/w. Up to this point, but not beyond it, the choice of a type with a higher p_c will raise the growth-rate.

This result and its relationship to alternative criteria for choosing technique has been clearly and neatly represented by Dr. Amartya Sen in a diagram† which in some respects I think I prefer to my own. Perhaps, however, it is safer to play with one's own toys than to borrow someone else's; and I will not reproduce it here, but will use instead an alternative illustration of my own.

The list of alternatives of which we spoke earlier could be represented by the following curve, in which it will be noticed

---

* With our assumption of a one-one relationship between units of capital equipment and of labour, irrespective of the *type* of equipment, it is indifferent whether we treat this as being the productivity of the machine or of the labour operating it. For most purposes, however, it is convenient to speak of this as the productivity of labour, which is itself affected by the technique with which labour works.

† Amartya Kumar Sen, 'Some Notes on the Choice of Capital Intensity in Development Planning', in *Quarterly Journal of Economics*, Nov. 1957, pp. 574-5.

that the p_i's and the p_c's stand in inverse relationship to one another, indicating the higher cost of the more productive types. The curve could be of various shapes. I have elsewhere suggested that the most reasonable supposition is that it is flatter than a rectangular hyperbola;* and it is perhaps unnecessary to repeat these reasons here. If this is the case, we can then derive from this curve another one, a peaked-shape curve relating p_c, not to p_i alone, but to the *product* of p_i and p_c. This latter

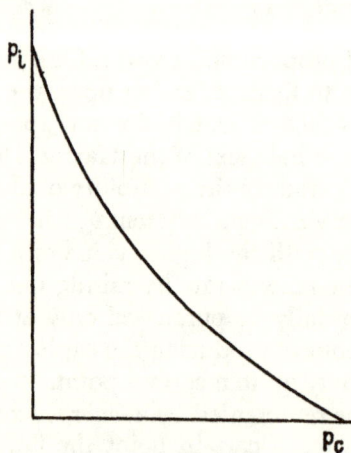

quantity, which is measured along the ordinate of the second diagram, represents the productivity of labour in the i-sector in terms of the final output-flow of the c-sector. It is thus a measure of Domar's σ (investment-productivity) when productivity is represented in terms of the final output-flow of consumer goods and investment in terms of labour. The abscissa of both diagrams, p_c, can be treated as an index of what is commonly called capital-intensity.

Manifestly the peak of the curve of the second diagram, where $p_i p_c$ attains its highest value, represents the minimum capital-output ratio (or maximum investment-productivity). It has an obvious attraction for commonsense as the position to aim at. And commonsense is right if to maximize output† and con-

* 'Second Thoughts on Capital-Intensity of Investment,' in *Review of Economic Studies*, vol. xxiv, 1956–7, no. 1, pp. 35–6.

† One can assume here that for purpose of measuring total output capital goods are valued in terms of an output-rate of consumer goods by applying to them the appropriate p .

sumption in the present is the proper objective of policy, as many have supposed it to be. But to do so will not maximize the growth-rate (save in the limiting case where $w=0$). $L_c.s/w$ will be maximized, and hence future investment potential, at a *higher* value of p_e than at the peak of the $p_i p_e$ curve—i.e. at some position on the downward slope to the right of the peak. This can be shown by adding to our diagram a series of secondary curves (those with the discontinuous lines), each appropriate to a particular level of w and relating p_e to p_i ($p_e - w$). It will be

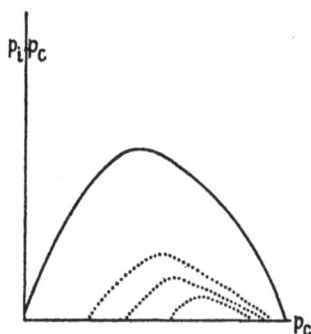

clear that the peaks of these curves must lie to the right of the peak of our main curve.* As we have seen, with a given labour force in the investment sector, it is on p_i that the size of dL_e/dt depends; and accordingly to maximize $p_i(p_e - w)$ will be to

maximize $\dfrac{dL_e \ (p_e - w)}{dt}$ and in turn dL_i /dt (whence also event-

ually dL/dt).

This criterion will evidently yield a higher capital-intensity, measured by p_e, the higher is w relatively to p_e (i.e. to the p_e of a particular technique or to the range of p_e's of all possible techniques). It might, therefore, seem that the theory of factor proportions has been justified after all. To the extent that the ratio of wages to productivity is determined by the supply of

* Alternatively this could be shown by including in our second diagram a series of $p_i w$ curves showing the values of p_i (as read off from the first diagram) multiplied by the appropriate values of w (a suggestion which I owe to Mr. L. L. Pasinetti). The position where tangents drawn to our $p_i p_e/p_e$ curve and to the appropriate $p_i w$ curve at a point vertically below are parallel will be one at which $p_i(p_e - w)$ is a maximum. (w is, of course, measured in the same product-units as is p_e.)

labour relatively to the means for employing labour, it is true
that this theory embodies an element of truth. On the other
hand, to the extent that the industrial wage-level, and *a fortiori*
the relation between productivity and wages, is governed by
other considerations than the labour supply, such as the subsistence requirements for maintaining a certain level of working
efficiency,* factor-proportions will fade out as an influence upon
the result. It is quite possible that the wage-productivity ratio
for any given technique (or the whole range of alternative
techniques) may be the same in a country where labour is dear
as in one where it is cheap, even though the labour supply
situation has an influence upon the absolute level of wages in
each case. In a socialist planned economy the chance of the
wage-level, and *a fortiori* the wage-productivity ratio, being to
a large extent independent of the supply situation of labour
seems to be greater than would otherwise be the case. This is
not to say that wage-*differentials* would not be related to the
labour-supply situation of different occupations (e.g. adjusted
so as to equalize at the margin the relative attractiveness of
occupations—Adam Smith's 'equalizing of net advantages');
but the *general* level of the wage structure as a whole might well
be, for social and incentive reasons, higher (in the conditions of
our model) than would be dictated by the supply situation of
labour as a whole.

To some, however, it may seem inherently irrational to choose
a technique that happens to maximize investment-potential in
preference to one that will maximize $p_i p_c$, when the former
makes total output and consumption smaller than they might
have been.† Such a view is perhaps quite natural to anyone
who sees the problem of efficient production in terms of allocating a certain supply of factors of production, with factor-
quantities treated as given and factor-prices as the unknowns of
the problem. Modern economists have travelled some distance
from the classical notion of 'productive consumption' involved
in labour (as in capital-replacement) and Ricardo's 'consumption necessary for production'. Once, however, we regard labour

---

* On this see H. Leibenstein, *op. cit.*, pp. 62–5.

† Cf. Professor R. F. Kahn's reference to using "available capital in a relatively
inefficient manner, i.e. less productively than it would be employed if it were used
with more labour", in 'The Pace of Development' in *The Challenge of Development*
(Hebrew University, Jerusalem, 1958), pp. 190–1, also 192–3.

as involving a certain necessary level of consumption and accordingly include this in our comparison of alternative output-totals, the apparent irrationality of choosing to maximize the *difference* between production and consumption if this will aid growth disappears.* True, consumption by workers, viewed as a social cost, cannot be treated as completely on a par with the replacement of raw materials or machinery used-up in production. At the same time, the fact that it is a condition, as well as an end, of economic activity cannot be ignored.

If alternatively the objective of policy is to afford the maximum employment at the earliest possible date, then it would appear that a point should be chosen as far to the left as possible on our curve, with a very low value of p_c and a high value of p_i. This would represent the production of a large number of very cheap capital goods of low productivity (e.g. Robert Owen's spade-husbandry). With a *given* available investment-fund it would involve immediately a larger increase in L_c than would any other position on the curve. However the low value of p_c would very soon react adversely on employment in the i-sector, L_i (i.e. as soon as the initial investment-fund had been used up). Take the extreme case where p_c is no higher than w: the absence of any surplus in the c-sector would make it impossible any longer to support workers in the i-sector; L_i would fall to zero and growth would stop. Thus to seek to maximize employment by moving down the left-hand slope of the curve would be a very short-sighted policy. Yet this seems to be a plausible implication of using (as some wish to do) a 'notional wage' of zero as an investment criterion in conditions where there is a surplus of labour. To maximize employment for any length of time one would have to stay at the peak of the curve (maximizing employment being equivalent to maximizing consumption).

It may be worth noting parenthetically that, whereas any of the positions to the *right* of the peak are capable of being chosen by *entrepreneurs* in a capitalist economy, according to the level of wages, positions down the *left*-hand slope of the curve, such as we have just been talking about, could not be chosen (unless

---

* The issue can, I think, be expressed in formal terms like this: to assume that wages have no positive minimum level (and hence can fall to zero) is equivalent to assuming in the case of other factors that their prices can have negative values, i.e. prices that do not permit of replacement.

it were by reason of ignorance or uncertainty). A capitalist *entrepreneur* faced with technical alternatives would presumably choose the most profitable (which would be that which yielded the highest ratio of surplus to original investment cost), and even if wages were to approach zero he would not move further left than the peak itself, since to the left of it both the rate of profit and total profit would get progressively smaller. (This is not, of course, to say that the choice would add as much to growth as would a similar choice of technique in a planned economy: that would depend on how much of the realized surplus was reinvested and how much of it claimed by the 'unproductive consumption' of a leisured class; and at any rate the choice of the most profitable position will only maximize growth if higher productivity raises the savings ratio, which, as we have seen, is in those conditions uncertain.) * Nor would the left slope represent possible positions under the factor-proportions theory unless this were to be so construed as to admit of negative factor-prices. † What we have called a short-period maximum-employment position could only be achieved by State investment, ignoring profit-considerations, or by subsidization of wages, having the form of a bonus proportional to the number of workers employed.

Manifestly there is a conflict between the humanitarian objective of providing employment to the maximum number of persons in the present or near future and the requirements of growth. It may well be that in any actual situation some compromise would have to be made between them and only a doctrinaire would insist on plumping for one objective. It may

---

* See above, p. 35. There are other qualifications to the statement that an *optimum* choice of technique from the standpoint of growth is identical with choice by private enterprise. There are well-known reasons why what is profitable to a single *entrepreneur* may not be the same as what maximizes profit for the whole class of *entrepreneurs*; and Professor R. F. Kahn has emphasized that where there is indirect taxation or whenever "a man who is provided with additional employment increases his consumption by less than the wage which he is now paid", there will be a divergence between the most profitable choice for private *entrepreneurs* and the socially *optimum* choice of technique (*op. cit.*, p. 190). There may also be divergence to the extent that there are monopoly-prices for products that are inputs of other industries or monopoly-inflated profit-margins in any industry.

† In terms of Dr. Sen's diagram that we have mentioned above (p. 37), they would be positions on the right-hand slope of the Q-curve; and it is immediately obvious on inspection that these could only qualify as most-profitable positions if the wage-line had a negative slope.

even be that inconsistent decisions would have to be made in different sectors of the economy, such as investing in fairly capital-intensive forms in industry while assisting the unemployed or unproductively employed to achieve at least the level of a subsistence economy by supplying them very cheaply with primitive equipment or materials—or, as the Indian Second Five Year Plan has done, investing simultaneously in modern steel plants and in cottage industry. To the extent that the labour force is non-homogeneous and labour immediately available for industrial employment is limited at any one date because a certain standard of skill and experience and type of social culture (possibly of nutrition) is there required, such apparent inconsistencies in policy may have a rational economic basis. Yet is this conflict between growth and employment, when we examine it, quite as real as superficially it appears to be? With a given current supply of consumer goods, the only real alternative at any given point of time is between employing fewer people at a higher wage and more at a lower wage. If to give more employment can only be done by a change in the forms of investment that is harmful to the expansion of the investment-potential, then it will not be very long before such a course entails a *lower* level of employment than would have resulted had this course not been adopted. In other words, the conflict is a real one to the extent that one focuses attention on the near future; and it disappears the further one looks ahead. There will be some date in the future beyond which the two rival objectives will fuse, and the course which maximizes growth (if pursued over the whole period from now to then) will also maximize employment at any given date. Analogous considerations, as we shall see later, apply to the conflict between investment and consumption, which may actually disappear at a much earlier date than is usually imagined. In our present context, however, this particular conflict is secondary, being subordinated to the conflict between investment and employment.*

* It is subordinated, that is, if we assume (as we have so far done) that the level of wages is a 'necessary' level (for whatever reason): cf. above, pp. 30, 40. The choice is then exclusively between more employment (and the consumption necessary to it) with less investment and less employment (and less consumption) but more of it in the investment sector (both absolutely and proportionately). Once, however, this assumption about wages is dropped one could have of course (up to a point) more employment (*and* more consumption) without any conflict with investment.

There is one type of decision that we have so far not considered, namely decisions about the period of production (in
the sense of the period of time elapsing between the start and
completion of a particular batch of output). Where this period
is not dictated by natural conditions (as with the harvest cycle)
it will be largely affected by technical conditions. Thus a change
of technique, besides altering productivity, may alter the actual
time-lags with which the process of growth operates.

In some cases, where the methods of production are sufficiently flexible, the period of production can be altered at will
(within fairly wide limits) merely by altering the degree of concentration of labour simultaneously employed upon a particular
piece of work. Perhaps the best examples come from constructional work: the making of a railway or a road or a canal or a
building can be extended over six months or six years according
to how much labour is employed on it; and a given cost in
man-days may be alternatively composed of few men working
many days or many men working relatively few days. In such
cases it might seem as though the period of production would
be quite arbitrary. It may well be, however, that to lengthen
the period has the advantage of yielding certain economies,
since to employ less labour simultaneously on any given project
(extending its employment instead over a larger stretch of time)
may ease the pressure on certain bottleneck-factors, thereby
reducing the total man-hour cost of the job and equivalently
raising the productivity of labour.*

* This would be an example of what is sometimes called 'short-period diminishing returns', and of the possibility of avoiding it by taking longer over any given
job, which implies that the proportion in which labour and equipment, etc., are
combined can be varied (a possibility excluded if we hold to the one-one assumption
made above). The economy in question would accordingly be relative to the stock
of capital equipment existing at any date in a given sector or industry; clearly there
can be no advantage in lengthening *per se*. A canal, for instance, could be built in
a much shorter time if a great deal of labour were concentrated upon it, but only
at the expense, probably, of much of this labour having to work with very inadequate equipment and hence unproductively; whereas to concentrate what equipment there was upon fewer men would raise average per man-hour productivity,
thus enabling the canal to be built with less man-hours in total, but stretched over
a longer time. Meantime the labour not occupied on the canal in the second case
could be used to start another one (or else a road or a railway), with some of this
labour making more equipment to be used on the second project. To the extent
that in the economy at large more equipment would be needed in the second case
to employ the labour force (which is what the economy of lengthening the period
comes down to), this question is necessarily associated with the problem we shall

Is there any corresponding advantage from shorter production periods to be set against the possible economies we have mentioned from taking more time? At first sight it is not obvious that there is, since the growth-rate, as we have seen, will depend, *ceteris paribus*, upon the productivities; and if these measured over any period are the same, or can even be raised by taking more time over any given batch of output, nothing would seem to be lost by lengthening the production period.

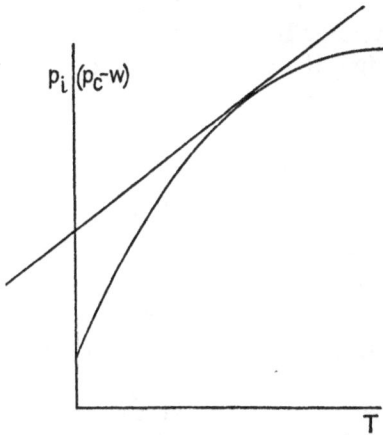

The answer lies in what may be called the 'compounding effect' of having any given increase of surplus, and hence investment-potential, at an earlier date, and consequently advancing to this earlier date the larger increment of production which this enhanced investment potential occasions. From the standpoint of growth, the best choice of production period will accordingly be that which causes the difference made to the compounding effect by a change of period to balance the difference made to surplus by enhanced productivity. This can be depicted graphically by a curve representing the values of $p_i(p_c - w)$ (measured along the ordinate) associated with different lengths of production period, or T (measured along the abscissa). Such a representation could be regarded as a third

discuss in Chapter IV; although it should be noted that the diversion of labour to enlarging the stock of equipment is mainly (though not entirely) a once-for-all diversion when the change is made to a longer period, not a continuing diversion.

dimension to our previous diagram on page 39 above. Presum
ably the advantage of higher productivity as one takes mor
time on any job will be a diminishing one, so that the curve i
question will be concave to the T-axis and gradually flatten-ou
to a summit-value of $p_i(p_c - w)$. If there were no compoundin
effect, this summit-value would be the appropriate one t
choose. The compounding effect, however, consisting as it doe
of a certain rate of increment of surplus per unit of time, can b
represented in familiar Wicksellian fashion by the slope of
line rising at a certain angle from the T-axis (projected nega
tively) of our diagram. Its point of tangency with the slope
the curve will define the optimum period of production, sinc
at this point

$$\frac{ds}{dt} = \frac{dp_i(p_c - w)}{dt}.$$

Thus ds/dt, depending *inter alia* upon the ratio p_c/w, will pla
the rôle in our model of a rate of discount in relation to an
decisions where time is involved (e.g. the example on p. 2
above).

A similar consideration may be relevant to the choice
technique if the difference of technique involves for any reaso
a substantial difference in the period of production. Let us tak
as an example what is coming to be known as the 'Chines
method' of using primitive local industries (e.g. tradition
'wheelbarrow' methods of dam-building or small locall
assembled blast-furnaces), which are highly labour-using b
because of the widely dispersed reserves of local labour can b
utilized very extensively in supplementation of the main (mo
technically advanced) construction projects. It is quite possibl
of course, for this type of development to result in an impressi
increase in gross production while the extension of employme
is taking place; but this is not to say that it will necessarily yie
an equivalently large surplus (since a very large proportion
the increase in gross production will represent an increase
wages). Here the principle we have enunciated above will st
apply: if there are alternative technical methods that yield
higher value of $p_i (p_c - w)$, then those methods will yield a high

future growth-rate than will this one*; and use of the latter could scarcely fail to reduce the growth-rate unless the additional employment in question involved no claim upon the investment fund of society (in the shape of the output and labour of the i-sector). † Where, however, it is possible that this 'Chinese method' might have an offsetting advantage is in having a shorter period of production, and hence contributing to the growth-rate *via* the compounding effect by shortening the time-lags of the process and having increments of investment at earlier dates. To say that this is possible is not to say that it is certain: to make such a comparison concrete evidence is needed. But such a possibility must always be borne in mind.

---

* It is, of course, possible that in such a case we should need to drop our simplifying assumption of a one-one relation between capital goods and the employment they involve when in use; in which case we should have to introduce into this condition an additional quantity such as the θ whose meaning is discussed below (Chap. IV, p. 50), and the appropriate maximand would then become $p_i \theta (p_c - w)$. Although for each worker the margin between p_c and w might be very narrow, the surplus yielded by all the workers employed by a particular capital good might be quite large.

† This condition would, for example, be fulfilled if any implements or materials used by this labour were capable of being made also by otherwise unemployed labour without fixed capital (i.e. labour that for some reason was incapable of being drawn into employment in the i-sector proper), and without occasioning additional consumption greater than the surplus production of the former group of workers.

IV

CHOICE OF TECHNIQUE IN THE INVESTMENT SECTOR: THE MODEL EXTENDED

A LIMITATION of the two-sector model as we have used it so far is that it takes no account of the production of capital goods for use in the investment sector itself. Thus we have been faced with a certain lack of symmetry; employment in the consumption goods sector being governed by the stock of capital equipment and its type and not at all by the wage, whereas employment in the investment sector was governed both by the level of wages and by the available 'subsistence fund', and was free to vary with any change in either. (Since we have assumed the wage-level to be constant, attention has been focused exclusively upon the second of these two factors.) This lack of symmetry did no harm, and was even a convenience, when we were concerned with the choice of technique in sector-c alone. Are the essentials of our analysis affected, however, if we complicate the picture by introducing fixed capital into the investment sector as well; and can we find any analogous criterion for the choice of technique in this sector?

Once we allow for fixed capital in the investment sector itself we shall have to adopt some parallel assumption about the 'technical coefficient' to the one-tractor-one-tractor-driver that we postulated above: for example, that each machine-tool needs one operator irrespective of its technical type. We shall also need to allow for the fact that the employment of additional labour in this sector requires as its pre-condition the production of an equivalent number of machines on which the labour can work; and that accordingly only *part* of its total labour force can be employed on manufacturing equipment for the c-sector and hence contributing directly to growth—another part must always be engaged on making machines for next year's new workers to work with. Obviously, the smaller the proportion of the i-sector labour force that is employed on this latter task, the larger *ceteris paribus* will be dL_c/dt. We could assume that such machines are themselves made with 'unassisted labour' in the i-sector; or we could assume (which we may as well do once we have started on this tack) that the machine-makers also need machines with which to work, and which in turn will need a portion of the i-sector labour force to make, and so on.

To handle this more complex situation we shall need to break down our investment sector into at least two sub-branches within it. Let us label these two branches i and m, the first as before being occupied with producing capital equipment for the c-sector and the second with producing machine-tools that can be used alternatively in making the capital equipment for the c-sector *or* in branch-m in making machine-tools themselves. This latter branch will accordingly be capable of a circular process of self-expansion, as well as of producing to meet the needs of expansion of branch-i. It can, however, only pursue this self-expansion process at the expense of diverting to itself some proportion* of the investment-sector labour-force that could otherwise have been making equipment for the c-sector and hence contributing directly to the growth-rate as measured by dL_c/dt.

We can then use L_i and L_m, p_i and p_m, for employment in each branch and for the productivity of labour in each (measured in terms of product-units of the outputs of the two branches respectively, say tractors and machine-tools). Where necessary we can refer to the labour-force of the whole investment sector as L_{i+m}; and we can also refer to the two distinct destinations of the output of branch-m (for itself and for branch-i) by writing L_{m1} and L_{m2}.

We shall then have the following structural equations†

* This may not and probably will not mean any absolute transfer: merely a shift in the proportional distribution of the annual intake of *new* labour between the branches of the investment-sector.

† These equations are similar in kind (if containing less detail regarding input, and lacking an explicit time-reference) to the 'structural conditions' of A. Lowe in *Capital Formation and Economic Growth* (Princeton, 1955), pp. 587 *seq.*; cf. also Ch. Bettelheim, *loc. cit.*, pp. 10–17.

governing employment in the branches of our investment sector:

$$L_i = \frac{dL_c}{dt} \cdot \frac{1}{p_i}$$

$$L_{m1} = \frac{dL_i}{dt} \cdot \frac{1}{p_{m1}}$$

$$L_{m2} = \frac{dL_{m1}}{dt} \cdot \frac{1}{p_{m2}}$$

(This third equation, as we shall see in a moment, is incomplete.) For *changes* in employment we can derive directly from the above these further ones (which are not additional conditions, of course, but implied in the others):

$$\frac{dL_i}{dt} = \frac{d^2L_c}{dt^2} \cdot \frac{1}{p_i} \text{ and } \frac{dL_{m1}}{dt} = \frac{d^2L_i}{dt^2} \cdot \frac{1}{p_{m1}}, \text{ etc.}$$

It will remain true, as in our simpler case in the last section, that

$$L_{i+m} = L_c \cdot \frac{s}{w} \text{ and } \frac{dL_{i+m}}{dt} = \frac{dL_c}{dt} \cdot \frac{s}{w}$$

The main thing that these equations tell us—and it is worth stressing since it will prove to be of major importance in the sequel—is that the distribution of labour between the branches will be different for every different growth-rate of the system, given the productivities; and for any given growth-rate this distribution will be different for every different set of values for the productivities. This distribution will be more favourable to growth, *ceteris paribus*, the larger is the ratio L_i/L_m, and *vice versa*; but at the same time this distribution cannot be treated as independent of the rate of growth when considering the determinants of the latter.

Two complications should perhaps be mentioned immediately. Were it not for our simplifying one-machine-one-man assumption, we should have to substitute for the $1/p_i$, etc. . . . which appears here something like θ_{ic}/p_i . . ., etc., where θ is a technical coefficient relating units of labour to a unit (or units) of equipment measured in product units of that equipment. What we are here doing is to treat θ throughout as $=1$, so that we can conveniently ignore it, and moreover ignore the possibility of its magnitude changing with changes in the type of equipment.

The second complication is a more serious one (and as we shall see more crucial for our problem). The equations governing L_m in its two categories, as we have expressed them, understate the necessary size of this branch. Unless we are to assume that labour in branch-m_2 works unassisted by fixed capital, L_{m_2} will have to be large enough to provide equipment for its own expansion as well as for the expansion of L_{m_1}. To state the position fully, therefore, we need to rewrite our equation for L_{m_2} as follows:

$$L_{m_2} = \frac{dL_{m_1}}{dt} \cdot \frac{1}{p_{m_2}} + \frac{d^2 L_{m_1}}{dt^2} \cdot \left(\frac{1}{p_{m_2}}\right)^2 + \frac{d^3 L_{m_1}}{dt^3} \cdot \left(\frac{1}{p_{m_2}}\right)^3 + \ldots$$

Accordingly the size of the labour force in the whole branch-m is likely to be large relatively to L_i, and will tend to become larger as the growth-rate rises. As in the simpler case of the last chapter, the growth-rate will essentially depend on $L_i p_i$ and s/w (although we can no longer deduce the size of L_i directly from the size of s/w). The effect of any change in p_i on the growth-rate is obvious. But what of the effect of p_m? The advantage of a high p_m is that *per se* it reduces the size of L_m relatively to L_i; hence its contribution to the growth-rate operates *via* its contribution to enlarging L_i. True, this contribution will be partly offset by the influence of a higher growth-rate on the distribution of labour between branch-i and branch-m. But this offset can be no more than partial. For example, if dL_i/dt is to be raised at all by the change, p_{m_1} must rise (and hence $1/p_{m_1}$ in our equation must fall) by a more than proportional amount; otherwise the size of L_{m_1} cannot fall relatively to L_i in consequence of the change. (The same applies, *mutatis mutandis*, to the influence of a change in dL_c/dt and in $d^2 L_c/dt^2$ occasioned by a change in p_i.)

It will be clear from the above structural equations that when the system is expanding at a constant (relative) rate of growth, the proportions in which labour is distributed between the branches of the investment sector (as well as between the i-sector as a whole and the c-sector) will remain constant; and for this to be so the relative growth-rates of all branches of the system must be equal, namely:

$$\frac{dL_c}{dt} \cdot \frac{1}{L_c} = \frac{dL_i}{dt} \cdot \frac{1}{L_i} = \frac{dL_{m1}}{dt} \cdot \frac{1}{L_{m1}} = \frac{dL_{m2}}{dt} \cdot \frac{1}{L_{m2}}$$

This will represent movement in what Mrs. Robinson terms 'golden age' conditions;* and our problem is to find the techniques that will make this constant growth-rate a maximum. If, however, either the growth-rate is changing, or technique and with it the relevant productivities are changing, then as we have seen these proportions will change also. This is of crucial importance to the choice of technique in branch-i, since to choose a more capital intensive technique (involving a more costly m_1-product), while it will have the beneficial effect of raising p_i and thence the growth-rate, will have the disadvantage of shifting the proportions in which the investment-sector labour force is distributed in the direction of branch-m (since more m-labour will now be required to produce the more costly m_1 products) to the detriment of branch-i.

The commonsense rule for choosing technique in branch-i in the interests of maximum growth is to move in the direction of higher capital intensity so long as its effect in raising p_i is greater than its effect in depleting L_i by shifting the proportions in which labour is distributed between the two branches (i and m). When this latter effect (due to the fall in p_{m1}) offsets the former (the rise in p_i), no further net gain from raising capital intensity in branch-i is possible. In other words, $L_i p_i$ will be maximized when

$$\frac{dp_i}{p_i} = -\frac{dL_i}{L_i}.$$

This in itself is an application of a quite obvious and familiar principle, to balance the cost in additional labour in the one branch against the benefit from higher labour-productivity in the other.

Does this commonsense precept enable us to deduce anything

* *Accumulation of Capital* (London, 1956), p. 99 *et seq.*

about the capital-intensity of technique in branch-i that will be most favourable to the growth-rate?

It is clear that any fall in p_{m1} occasioned by transition to a more costly type of m_1-product will need to be compensated by an (approximately) equi-proportional increase in the labour force of branch-m_1 if the output of m_1-products (measured in physical units) is to be maintained. This increase in L_{m1}, which can only be met by a transfer from L_i,* will involve a fall in L_i which expressed as a *proportion* of L_i (i.e. as $\Delta L_i / L_i$) will be large or small comparatively according as L_i is small or large relatively to L_{m1}. If, but only if, the ratio L_i / L_{m1} were equal to unity would the transfer involve an equi-proportional rise of L_{m1} and fall of L_i; in which case one could define the position (in the range of alternative techniques) where $L_i p_i$ was a maximum as being that at which

$$\frac{-dp_{m1}}{p_{m1}} = \frac{dp_i}{p_i}.$$

But this would be a special case only of a more general condition for $L_i p_i$ being maximized, namely:

$$\frac{-dp_{m1}}{p_{m1}} = \frac{dp_i}{p_i} \cdot \frac{L_i}{L_{m1}}.$$

If we assume a similar type of relationship between changes in p_i and changes (of opposite sign) in p_{m1} as was depicted in our diagrams in Chapter III for p_c and p_i, it follows that a more capital-intensive technique should be chosen the larger is L_i / L_{m1}, and conversely.

The size of L_i / L_{m1} depends, as we have seen, upon the rate of growth and upon the size of the relevant productivities: that is, upon dL_i / dt and upon p_{m1}; being smaller (and hence the optimum capital intensity of i-technique lower) the higher the growth-rate and the larger is p_{m1}.

To simplify our analysis, let us start by assuming that in the neighbourhood of the optimum position all the p's in the investment sector are approximately equal to unity, so that we may

---

* It can only be met at the expense of L_i because the *total* labour-force of the investment sector is fixed at any given date by the condition that:

$$\frac{L_i + L_{m1} + L_{m2}}{L_c} = \frac{s}{w}$$

ignore their influence upon the distribution of labour within the sector. The size of the labour-force in any one branch relatively to the labour-force in the next branch will then be governed exclusively by the growth-rate. Since our structural equations yield these equalities:

$$L_i = \frac{dL_c}{dt} \left(\text{ignoring } \frac{1}{p_i} = 1\right)$$

$$\frac{dL_i}{dt} = \frac{d^2L_c}{dt^2}, \ L_{m1} = \frac{dL_i}{dt}, \ \frac{L_i}{L_c} = \frac{L_{m1}}{L_i}$$

and since (with $p_i = 1$) $\frac{L_i}{L_c} = \frac{dL_c}{dt} \cdot \frac{1}{L_c}$, which is the proportional

growth-rate; then, writing the latter as G, we have the following:

$$\frac{L_i}{L_c} = \frac{L_{m1}}{L_i} = G.$$

By analogy we can infer (recalling what was said earlier about the size of L_{m2}) that

$$L_{m2} = L_{m1} \cdot \sum_{n=1}^{\infty} G^n.$$

We already know that

$$\frac{L_i + L_{m1} + L_{m2}}{L_c} = \frac{s}{w}.$$

It follows from this and the two preceding equations that

$$\frac{L_c \cdot \sum_{n=1}^{\infty} G^n}{L_c} = \frac{s}{w}.$$

Remembering that $\sum_{n=1}^{\infty} G^n = \frac{G}{1-G}$, we can derive the follow-

ing value for G:*

---

* There is, indeed, an alternative and perhaps more direct way of arriving at $s/(s+w)$ as the value of G, which may seem intuitively obvious to readers who have seen all the implications of this model. Since $L_{i+m}/L_c = s/w$, $s/(s+w)$ can be seen to represent the rate of investment measured in terms of labour: i.e. $L_{i+m}/$

$$G = \frac{s}{s+w}$$

Let us now return to our condition defining the optimum choice of technique for branch-i. Since $\frac{L_i}{L_{m1}} = \frac{1}{G} = \frac{s+w}{s}$, we can rewrite that condition (page 53 above) in this way:

$$\frac{-dp_{m1}}{p_{m1}} = \frac{dp_i}{p_i} \cdot \frac{s+w}{s}.$$

By analogy with our second diagram in Chapter III we can depict the relationship between $p_{m1}p_i$ and p_i by the following

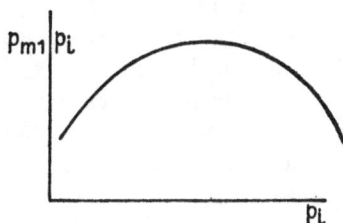

curve. Here again the abscissa, along which in this case p_i is measured, is the index of capital-intensity.

The condition for $p_{m1}p_i$ to be at a maximum is that

$$\frac{-dp_{m1}}{p_{m1}} = \frac{dp_i}{p_i}.$$

It is clear that the optimum condition as we have restated it could only reduce to such an equality in the case where $w = 0$ and consequently $G = 1$ (with the total labour-force concen-

---

$(L_{i+m} + L_c)$. If the p's are uniform, it will also represent the rate of investment in terms of *product*. But if p_i and p_m are both unity, then on the assumptions of our model the rate of investment is *ipso facto* the rate of growth (it may be recalled that we are assuming all branches of the system, and hence all products, to be growing at the same rate, when the system is in equilibrium, so that no 'weighting' problem affects this result).

To assume that the p's, besides being uniform, are equal to unity may be regarded, indeed, as equivalent to choosing a time-period that will make the rate of growth equal to the rate of investment (the values of p and G alike varying with the unit-period chosen).

trated upon branch-m_2 of the investment sector). Only in such a case could the peak of our curve be chosen. In all cases where w is positive, our condition defines a point on the curve to the *right* of the peak, and further to the right (signifying greater capital-intensity) the larger is w in relation to s. Thus we reach the not-uninteresting conclusion that the choice of technique in the investment sector is dependent on the surplus-ratio (i.e. s/w) in the consumption (or wage-goods) sector.

Can we say anything more about the relationship between technique in the two sectors? If we assume a precise correspondence between our two sets of curves, relating respectively p_{m_1} to p_i and p_i to p_c * (which is equivalent to assuming that the cost-situation for producing machines of given productivity is alike in the two cases), then it can be shown that the degree of capital-intensity (as measured respectively by p_i and p_c) will be the same in the two situations—still ignoring any influence of the productivities upon the labour-distribution.

The optimum choice of technique in sector-c as we defined it in Chapter III was where $p_i(p_c - w)$ was maximized instead of $p_i p_c$. It will be evident that the relationship between the higher $p_i p_c$ curve and the lower $p_i(p_c - w)$ curve can be expressed thus:

$$\frac{p_i p_c}{p_i(p_c - w)} = \frac{p_c}{p_c - w}.$$

But $\frac{p_c}{p_c - w} = \frac{s + w}{s}$. Accordingly the point on the higher $p_i p_c$ curve vertically above the peak of the lower $p_i(p_c - w)$ curve can be defined as

$$\frac{-dp_i}{p_i} = \frac{dp_c}{p_c} \cdot \frac{s + w}{s}$$

which is the same, *mutatis mutandis*, as the condition defining technical choice in branch-i. The significance of $(s + w)/s$ is, of course, that it is the measure of the degree to which s is increased proportionally by a given proportionate rise in p_c.†

---

* For a justification of the procedure of treating independently the curve relating p_{m_1} and p_i and the earlier curve for the c-sector, see below, pp. 59–60.

† See further below, p. 95.

Obviously an analogous argument to what has been used in
the case of m_1-products for branch-i could be applied to the
choice of technique in branch-m_1 (m_2-products used in m_1), and
correspondingly to the choice of technique in branch-m_2 itself.
(In the latter case one would need to distinguish between (a) the
varying cost of making various types of m_2-product of varying
productivity *by means of* a given type of m_3-product, and (b) the
varying cost of making a given type of m_2-product *by means of*
varying types of m_3-product.)

The neatness of our conclusion about choice of technique in
the investment sector is disturbed as soon as we reintroduce the
influence of the productivities on labour distribution by drop-
ping the assumption that these are uniformly equal to unity.
The formula for the growth-rate, as derived by Mr. Johansen
and Dr. Ghosh in their Note to this Chapter, now becomes
(taking p_m as an average productivity for branch-m):

$$G = \frac{p_i p_m s}{p_i s + p_m w}.$$

There is now nothing to prevent G from being equal to or
greater than unity even if w is positive. However, the relation
between the labour-force in i and c and between the labour-
force in m_1 and i is no longer equal to G, but to G divided by
the values of the relevant productivities. Thus

$$\frac{L_i}{L_c} = \frac{G}{p_i} \quad \text{and} \quad \frac{L_{m1}}{L_i} = \frac{G}{p_{m1}}$$

and similarly

$$L_{m2} = L_{m1} . \sum_{n=1}^{\infty} \left(\frac{G}{p_{m2}}\right)^n$$

An examination of the equation defining G will show that, when
p_i and p_m have uniform values,* their influence on G will be of
the order of their own separate magnitudes. Consequently, since
this magnitude will be present both in the numerator and in the

---

* Fairly uniform values are not so improbable as they might at first seem to be;
since, although choice of a capital-intensive technique in sector-c will depress p_i,
choice of a similar technique in branch-i will tend to raise it equivalently. Correspondingly the depressing effect of the latter upon p_m will be counteracted by the
choice of technique of similar capital-intensity in branch-m.

denominator of the fraction which defines the relationship between L_i and L_{m1} (as between L_{m1} and L_{m2}) it will still follow that

$$\frac{L_i}{L_{m1}} = \frac{s+w}{s}$$

The only case that is likely to give trouble is where there is considerable diversity between the magnitudes of p_i and p_m; and then it will only qualify seriously the conclusion we have reached about capital-intensity where p_i is appreciably larger than is p_m. The economic content of such a case seems to be that the cost of producing *m*-products of any type and degree of productivity is sufficiently great, compared with cost-conditions in subsequent stages of production, as to make it worth-while to economize as much as possible on these products and to avoid putting the more costly types into production. It may be noted that a disparity between p_m and p_i represents a divergence from the average of the capital-labour ratio in branch-i (as measured by the ratio of L_{m1} to L_i): the only way in which the capital-labour ratio can vary in terms of our model.

Save in this case, our conclusion that the optimum choice of technique will lie to the right of the peaks of our $p_{m1}p_i/p_i$ or $p_{m2}p_{m1}/p_{m1}$ curves (above, page 55) remains undisturbed. Though modified by the influence of the productivities, to the extent (and only to the extent) that these are not uniform, this choice will still depend primarily on the surplus-ratio in the c-sector, the appropriate degree of capital-intensity being higher the smaller is s/w. Thus the influence of the productivities does not qualify our previous conclusions about capital intensity in the investment sector as much as at first it seemed likely to do.

It may be noted that once the appropriate choice of technique has been made, there will be no reason to change it as the investment sector gets larger and growth proceeds (provided that this continues at a constant rate), except under the impact of progress in technical knowledge which extends the range of technical possibilities available.

An apparent difficulty in our analysis, as this has been conducted, may be mentioned, in order to make clear to anyone to whom it may have occurred that the difficulty is no more than apparent. At first sight one might think that the inter-dependence of the sectors of our model was such as to upset the results of analysing the conditions for choice of technique in each sector severally and independently, as has been done in this and the preceding chapter. Thus, to take our analysis of technical choice in sector-c: once we introduce the problem of fixed capital in the i-sector we have to count as one of the off-setting costs of a higher growth-rate the diversion of a larger proportion of the labour-force of the investment sector towards branch-m, with an equivalently smaller proportion left available in branch-i to contribute directly to the expansion of L_c, and hence of $L_c.s/w$. In assessing the advantage of raising p_c by improved technique in the c-sector do we not have to set against it the consequential shift in distribution of the investment sector labour-force, adding this to the debit side alongside the fall in p_i?

On reflection this difficulty can be seen to be an imaginary one for the following reason. For a rise in p_c to have an enduring effect on the growth-rate, this can only be *via* an increase of L_i. If there is no increase in L_i, the growth-rate cannot rise, and there can be no consequential shift in labour distribution within the investment sector. Hence the adverse effect of the latter on the size of L_i cannot be treated as detracting from the favourable effect on the growth-rate of an increase of surplus in sector-c; and what maximizes the latter will still maximize the growth-rate (even if at a lower level of the latter than might seem to follow in the simpler case examined in Chapter III).*

One could put this argument in another way, in terms made familiar by the reasoning of the present chapter.   It is true that with fixed capital in the investment sector any given rise in s/w, such as is occasioned by a rise of p_c, will only contribute to the growth-rate to the extent that it raises $s/(s+w)$. But it is also true that anything which maximizes $p_i.s/w$ will also maximize

$$\frac{p_i s}{p_i s + w} \text{ (and hence with } p_m \text{ independently given } \frac{p_i \cdot p_m s}{p_i s + p_m w} \text{).}$$

It may further be asked whether one can consider the choice

* *Seem* to follow since one could hardly assume as high a level of p_i if tractors were made with 'unassisted labour' (the assumption in Chapter III) as if they were made with the aid of machine-tools (the assumption of the present chapter).

of technique in the investment sector without taking account of possible reactions on the conditions governing choice of technique in the c-sector. Here again there is no reason to suppose that any real difficulty arises. The effect of any shift of technique in the investment sector will be to alter p_i or else L_i. But choice of technique in sector-c is concerned solely with the relationship between *changes* in p_c and *changes* in p_i as the type of i-product changes; and it is difficult to see why this relationship should change because p_i is altered by an alteration in the type of *m*-product supplied to branch-*i*. In other words, there is no reason to suppose that normally the proportional change in p_i will not be the same for *all* c-techniques (or i-products); in which case it can be regarded as raising or lowering the *level* of the p_i/p_c curve (above, pp. 38–9), while leaving unaltered the value of p_c at which the curve of the second diagram attains its peak. Thus the change can be treated as simply a change of scale along the ordinate of the diagram.* There would appear, accordingly, to be no difficulty about making an assumption of independence to the extent of discussing the choice of technique in the investment sector on the assumption that technique in the c-sector is already given.

So far we have devoted little attention to the peculiarities of branch-m_2 of the investment sector other than to regard it as a convenient box into which to pack all the residual production of machine-tools needed to equip both the expanding intake of new labour into branch-m_1 and the consequential expansion of its own labour-force. Thus its own production was never larger than was required to meet the demands of expansion in the investment sector at a constant rate. There is a peculiarity, however, of branch-m_2 upon which we have touched and which deserves emphasis: namely that it can constitute a circular production-process of its own, turning out machines capable of

* Similarly in Dr. Sen's diagram (*loc. cit.*, p. 574) a change in conditions of production in sector-i (his Dept. I) would simply have the effect of altering the scale of the top half of his diagram. The given investment would show for each of the degrees of capital intensity considered a shift in the employment created; this being expressed (in the case of a rise) by a shift of the three L_c points to the right, and an equivalent rise together with a rightward shift of the Q-curve (each point on which would move along its appropriate P-line). The point on this Q-curve at which a tangent to it was parallel to the wage-line would represent the same capital-intensity as before.

reproducing themselves, and also of reproducing, if need be, improved types of themselves, costlier to make in all probability but yielding when in use a higher p_m than their forbears. As such, branch-m_2 is capable of breaking out of the determinism laid upon it by our structural equations. The question immediately arises as to why it should not do so. These structural equations embody the relations of the familiar 'accelerator', but in this model (since we have conceived it in the context of a planned economy) they operate as the accelerator-relation *in reverse*, showing end-uses as dependent on the supply-conditions of capital goods, instead of the converse. It would seem quite natural, accordingly, to think of a build-up of capital goods as taking a lead in the process and providing the impetus to growth.

It is true that so far we have placed exclusive emphasis on putting as much of the investment-potential as possible into the consumer goods sector, so as to encourage the maximum rate of expansion of the surplus product of that sector. But it may well be asked: what of the alternative possibility of concentrating the investment-potential instead upon the self-reproducing process of m_2? In this way all the labour available to the investment sector would be progressively drawn into m_2 and concentrated there in using machine-tools of a cheaper type but inferior productivity to produce more expensive types of much higher productivity. The p_m appropriate to producing the new, more 'advanced', machines by means of the older machines would be considerably lower than the p_m appropriate to reproducing the *old* machines by means of the old machine; and accordingly there would be an initial period during which output declined measured in product-units. The advantage would be that once there were enough of the new (most productive known) types to replace the old, p_m would be greatly raised: i.e. raised above that prevailing in the initial position (otherwise there would be no advantage in altering the type). From then on both machines of the more productive type and labour could be exported again to branch-m_1 and branch-i, and thenceforth not only would p_i be higher but a smaller proportion of the investment labour force would need to be locked-up in branch-m to support any given growth-rate than would otherwise have been the case.

What would have been lost by this procedure is the chance of progressively enlarging the total investment labour force during the interval by enlarging the c-sector surplus. In the initial period the growth of consumption and employment would be nil. If *m*-products are reckoned in 'corrected' product-units to allow for their higher potential productivity, then the growth of output in the investment sector will be smaller or larger than otherwise according to whether dp_m/dt* is smaller or larger than $dL_c/dt \cdot s/w$; and the likelihood of the former being the larger will be greater the higher is w relatively to p_c (since $s = p_c - w$) and the lower the original values of p_i and p_m. The likelihood of the growth-rate of output as a whole being greater in this initial period is manifestly very small. In the subsequent period however the general growth-rate will be higher as a result of this procedure than it would have been if no priority had been given to the expansion of *m*-production. Since we are now faced with two different growth-rates, for the earlier period and the later, we cannot speak of one course of action as being better than the other from a growth-standpoint irrespective of a postulated terminal date; and there may well be different answers for different time-horizons.†

It remains to enquire what will be the effect of removing the assumption of an unexhausted reserve of labour on which we have been relying hitherto. Once this reserve is exhausted it is no longer possible to increase L_i and L_c simultaneously, and as the stock of capital in the c-sector increases as a result of current investment, an increasing proportion of it must go unused unless L_c is able to grow at the expense of L_i. Hence the investment sector and with it the growth-rate must decline, except in so far as it is maintained by technical progress, extending the possibilities for using more productive labour-saving techniques. For a

* This will depend essentially on the length of time it will take a worker operating an old-type machine to produce one machine of the most productive technical type in replacement of the former.

† Professor H. G. Johnson's demonstration in his 'Notes on Economic Development and Maximum Rate of Growth' in the *Malayan Economic Review*, April 1957, does not apply directly to the case we are considering, since it does not contemplate an increase in p as a result of concentrating resources on the investment sector. The lesson which Professor Johnson's demonstration seems to hold is that failure to use investible resources to increase employment in the consumption sector at the earliest possible date forfeits the compounding-advantage of ploughing back the surplus in expansion of the investment-potential; and this we have seen is a crucial consideration to be included in the balance when comparing the two development paths. Without the possibility of raising p_m there would be nothing to be said for concentrating investible resources on branch-m.

time, even without any progress in technical *knowledge*, investment and the growth-rate may be maintained (and the fall in L_{i+m} retarded) by using the investment-sector labour-force to raise technique in both sectors to the highest-known technical type: i.e. to a higher degree of capital intensity than that corresponding to our earlier criterion. When this process has been completed and productivity raised to the maximum extent, then (unless progress of technical knowledge is very rapid) the investment sector must begin exporting labour as well as capital goods to the consumption goods sector. In the process w must rise, thereby diminishing the s/w ratio in sector-c as the ratio of L_i to L_c falls; otherwise there would be a problem of unsold production in the consumer goods sector. The wage-level, in other words, can no longer have the rôle of an independent variable in the system.

As the supply of capital goods to the consumer goods sector continues, though at a slackening rate, in face of labour scarcity, there may arise a problem of redundancy of capital equipment as the declining investment sector and the growing consumer goods sector compete for labour. This redundancy will place a premium on scrapping plant and equipment—scrapping which will eventually become desirable in order to replace old equipment of lower productivity with new equipment of the most productive type; the pace of this substitution of new for old being governed by the state of labour scarcity, which will in turn be dependent on the rate of decline of the investment sector (varying inversely with the latter). This latter will be governed by the condition that the continuing rate of output of branch-i of the investment sector over any period must be sufficient to equip the amount of labour that the investment sector is exporting to the c-sector during that period.*

The process will end when net investment has fallen to zero, and (on our assumption of replacement being in normal circumstances zero) the whole labour force is employed in sector-c. Wages will absorb the whole product and s/w will be zero. In practice, however, approach to this type of 'long-run stationary state', as to others, will be indefinitely postponed as long as progress in technical knowledge is occurring.

* Some time-lag is inevitable; but ideally this should be as small as possible.

V

DISTRIBUTION OF INVESTMENT
BETWEEN THE SECTORS:
A CHANGE OF ASSUMPTION

IN introducing the problem of fixed capital in the investment
sector, as we did in the last chapter, we were virtually introducing a second investment-determinant; the growth-rate
being the resultant of balancing the rival claims of the two
determinants. Without the need to augment the supply of equipment in step with the intake of new labour into the investment
sector, the whole of the investment potential at any time could
have been directed towards expanding the consumption sector
and its surplus and hence the rate of increase of the investment-
potential. On the other hand the diversion of too large a part of
the i-sector labour force towards building up its own productive
capacity would have been at the expense of a reduced rate of
expansion of the c-sector and its surplus and hence a reduced
rate of growth of the investment-potential. Freedom from either
of the two determinants gives rein to a higher rate of growth,
ceteris paribus. We began our analysis (in Chapter III) with only
one determinant. I want now to revert to the case of one determinant, but this time in order to relax the first and to focus
attention upon the second.

Let us now assume that the main determinant of the rate of
investment is the output-capacity of the productive equipment
already installed in the sector of industry that makes capital
goods (e.g. steelmaking capacity, or the capacity of the engineering industry); and that the amount of labour that this sector can
absorb is limited by this factor and no longer by the supply of

wage-goods. (We could imagine, for example, either that real wages are flexible or that there are possibilities of an import surplus or of a favourable movement of the terms of trade with an agricultural economy outside the system that we are considering.) As a limiting factor upon investment and growth this is probably more prominent in a developed industrialized country than in an underdeveloped one; although even in the latter the dimensions of a development plan may be crucially affected by its existing steel capacity or by its ability to import machinery from elsewhere. *

In the degree to which we place emphasis on this investment determinant, the decision which matters for the growth-rate is that concerning the distribution of investment between the two sectors. This, indeed, may deserve more attention than the size of investment (whether measured absolutely or as a proportion of the national income) at some initial date; since the more that investment is used to expand the capacity of the capital goods sector of industry, the more rapidly can the investment-potential grow, in relation both to itself and to total output. From this standpoint investment devoted to the capital goods sector will have a growth-inducing influence which investment in the consumer goods sector will lack: it will contribute to the cumulative expansion of the investment-potential of the economy; which is quite the contrary conclusion to the one we have relied on hitherto.

It should be unnecessary to point out that the question of choice of technical form for any particular investment and the question of how investment is to be distributed between the two sectors are quite distinct issues of investment policy. Both in economic theory and in economic discussion, however, they seem at times to have been confused; perhaps because a raising of the capital-output ratio in any particular case and putting a larger proportion of an investment total into the capital goods sector have been regarded alike as altering the 'time-structure

* Cf. the following: ". . . the level of capital formation that a country can attain at any given time depends significantly on the size of the capital goods industry it has already built . . . if a backward country wishes quickly to attain a high rate of progress, what is necessary is not simply capital formation, but capital formation directed to the capital goods industries." (M. Abramowitz in *A Survey of Contemporary Economics*, vol. ii, ed. Bernard F. Haley, American Economic Association, 1952, p. 156.)

of investment' in the direction of 'earlier stages'.* I hope that it will become clear in what follows that these are issues to which different considerations apply; and that a decision to devote a large (or small) proportion of investment to capital goods industries by no means implies that one must choose a high (or low) degree of capital intensity for particular investment projects.

It is perhaps more convenient in this chapter to change the notation we have used hitherto, whereby we have spoken of the two sectors of our model as the i-sector and the c-sector, and instead to follow Marx's usage in speaking of sector 1 (means of production or capital goods) and sector 2 (consumer goods), if only because we are now dealing with a problem to which his well-known departmental schema most directly applies.† We can then use C_1, C_2 for the existing stock of capital equipment in the two sectors, and Y_1 and Y_2, I_1 and I_2 for the output and investment respectively in the two sectors. It seems convenient to use C, Y and I without subscript for total capital, output and investment, so that $C_1 + C_2 = C$, and similarly $I_1 + I_2 = I = \Delta C$. For simplicity we shall assume the capital-output ratio (C/Y) to be the same in both sectors and to be constant over time, and the investment-output ratio $(I/\Delta Y)$ to be equal to it.

If we write φ for the proportion of investment devoted to sector 1‡ (so that $I_1 = \varphi I$ and $\varphi = I_1/I$), then there will evidently be a critical value of φ at which growth proceeds at a constant (proportional) rate. This critical value of φ will be when it equals C_1/C, since then $I_1/C_1 = I_2/C_2 = I/C$, and C_1/C will have no tendency to change. When the capital-output ratio is the same in both sectors, C_1/C is the same as the rate of investment, I/Y (provided that capacity is fully utilized).§ Since the

---

* Cf. the present writer's remarks in *Review of Econ. Studies*, loc. cit.

† With the qualification that, like Professor P. C. Mahalanobis (in *Sankhya*, 1953 (Vol. 12), Part 4, p. 308), we are here assuming that "raw materials for consumer goods are included in the consumer goods industries", and not in sector 1.

‡ This is equivalent to Professor Mahalanobis's λ_i (*ibid.*, p. 309), and also, as we shall see below, to Domar's γ.

§ When the capital-output ratio differs in the two sectors,

$$\frac{C_1}{C} \text{ will} = \frac{K_1 I}{K_1 I + K_2 (Y - I)},$$

where K_1 and K_2 are the capital-output ratios of the two sectors respectively. If we derive therefrom the average capital-output-ratio for both sectors (which we will call simply K), the relationship can be expressed more simply as: $I/Y = C_1/C . K/K_1$. Cf. the present writer's 'Some Questions on Economic Growth' in *Indian Journal of Economics*, July 1955, p. 8.

growth-rate of income is equal to the rate of investment divided by the investment-output ratio (namely, $I/Y \mathbin{/} I/\Delta Y$), it follows that the growth-rate of output will in these circumstances remain unchanged.

If, however, φ is greater than C_1/C (which is equivalent to saying that it is greater than the current rate of investment—the 'savings-ratio' of Harrod-Domar equations), the growth-rate will be an increasing one:

$$\frac{I_1}{C_1} \text{ will be } > \frac{I}{C}; \frac{\Delta Y_1}{Y_1} \text{ will be } > \frac{\Delta Y}{Y};$$

consequently I/C, I/Y and $\Delta Y/Y$ will all rise.* The converse will be the case if φ is below the critical level: in this case the growth-rate must fall.

It will be clear from the way in which we have defined the critical value of φ that this is something determined by past history, which has brought the productive capacities of the two sectors to the relationship in which they now stand to one another. And if it is the product of past history, it will also change in the course of development, according to the way in which the investment-pattern alters the relative sizes of the two sectors (and hence the ratio C_1/C). Thus if φ is maintained above its critical value, this very fact will cause the critical value itself to rise, and to rise the more rapidly the more this coefficient exceeds the ratio C_1/C. This, as we have seen, is the same thing as saying that investment will rise as a proportion of total output. The converse, of course, is true if φ is maintained for a period below the existing ratio C_1/C: this very discrepancy will reduce the latter ratio and tend in the course of time to restore the two to equality. This means that a high value of φ can only promote a rising growth-rate temporarily, since it acts as itself a magnet to the very ratio that it is trying to exceed. To maintain a rising growth-rate, it has *itself to be rising over time*; and to this there is, of course, a definite ceiling when φ has reached unity, even if no lower ceiling is imposed by other considerations. This is to say no more than commonsense would expect: that it will

---

* In these circumstances I will increase at a rate equal to φ divided by the capital-output coefficient in sector 1; and consumption will rise by

$$\frac{I(1-\varphi)}{Y-I} \cdot \frac{1}{K_2}.$$

However, $I/(Y-I)$ will be rising, and in the course of time the growth-rates of both C and Y will rise until they are equal to the growth-rate of I.

become progressively more difficult to boost the growth-rate by boosting the relative size of the capital goods sector.

In practice, of course, there is likely to be a ceiling upon φ much lower than $\varphi = 1$. This ceiling will be imposed by the need to increase the output of consumer goods by enough to provide consumption goods for the additional workers employed in both sectors. This ceiling, be it noted, will be higher the more labour-saving the technique that is in use, since a given rate of investment will then involve a smaller growth of employment. But since this will mean (unless it is balanced by an equivalently high level of labour productivity) a higher capital-output ratio, the growth-rate yielded by a given rate of investment and a given φ* will be equivalently less. But the same general principle will still apply to technical choice as we discussed earlier: namely, that the labour-saving advantage of raising the ceiling on φ must be counted among the advantages of more capital-intensive technique; and it is misleading to balance simply the increased capital cost against the additional *output* this will yield.

It is at this stage that one can most conveniently ask the question as to the relationship in which what we have just been saying stands to our previous model. We are now looking at things from the reverse side. We regard the ceiling on φ as being imposed by the minimum rate of expansion of sector 2 that is needed to supply the consumption needs of the additional workers employed; whereas before we treated φ (which under conditions of constant proportional growth $= \dfrac{I}{Y} = \dfrac{L_{i+m}}{L_{i+m} + L_c}$) as determined by the ratio of surplus to wages in the consumer goods sector.† We can look on our previous model as a limiting case of our present one,‡ when φ has reached its ceiling, and

---

* To be precise this should read 'a given excess of φ over its critical value'.

† In so far as φ diverges from its critical value, it will be (on the assumption of uniform labour-productivities in the branches of the investment sector) equal to $\Delta L_m/(\Delta L_m + \Delta L_i)$.

We have seen that in equilibrium with constant growth

$$\frac{dL_m}{dt} \cdot \frac{1}{L_m} = \frac{dL_i}{dt} \cdot \frac{1}{L_i}$$

‡ Just as, conversely, the present one can be looked upon as a limiting case of the previous model. In their Notes to Chapter IV, Mr. Johansen and Dr. Ghosh point out that as the wage-rate approaches zero the growth-rate approaches p_m, productivity in the machine-building branch of the investment sector (this being explained by the fact that in these circumstances φ would rise to unity and the whole labour-force would be employed in branch-m).

its critical value has had time to rise to equality with itself so
that the growth-rate is constant. At the same time the possibilities have been exhausted of raising the ceiling on φ by labour-
saving changes in technique without retarding the growth-rate
more by increasing the capital-output ratio than further rises in
φ will accelerate it. The degree of freedom to vary φ that we
have been assuming until now has vanished.

What has essentially placed a restriction on our new model
and made it correspond to the old one is the premise that the
output of consumer goods must increase in the same proportion
as employment; accordingly, unless the capital-output ratio is
rising, the output-capacity of sector 2 must expand as fast as
investment. This is to reintroduce the assumption of a constant
real wage, and with it our other investment-determinant. The
importance to be attached to variations in our φ-coefficient as a
determinant of the growth-rate can, therefore, be seen to depend
on whether this assumption is a realistic one*; or. to put it in
terms of planning policy, on whether it can be regarded as ex-
pedient (from either an efficiency standpoint or a political one)
or socially desirable to permit some reduction in the real wage.
This is connected again with the question we mentioned earlier
about the determination of a minimum 'floor' to the industrial
wage (possibly a different 'floor' for different levels of efficiency)
and how inflexible this minimum is. The answer may well differ
according to the level of development that has already been
attained. To raise the growth-rate by increasing φ, since it
means increasing employment faster than the output of consumer goods, must mean a fall of consumption per employed
worker not merely temporarily but permanently, even though
the growth-rate ceases after a time to rise and is stabilized at the
higher level. Even though from then on the output of consumer
goods were to keep in step with employment, the former would
never catch up on the arrears. If φ were raised not once-for-all
but in a continuing ascent, consumption per employed worker
would *continue* to fall. A possible line of policy would be to allow
real wages to fall for a period in the interests of a rapid initial

* This bears a formal analogy with the part played in Mr. Kaldor's growth-
model by the assumption that the level of wages is "higher than the minimum set
by the supply-price of labour"; the case where wages are not higher being treated
as one where investment is governed by "the surplus over subsistence wages".
('A Model of Economic Growth' in *Economic Journal*, Dec. 1957, pp. 607–9.)

building-up of the investment potential, and then raise real wages again by lowering φ when development, with more equipment, had acquired greater momentum. But this would involve a slackened rate of growth at this later period (if φ were lowered below the critical level = the prevailing ratio of C_1/C).

This is to abstract, of course, from progress in technical knowledge; and if this were fast enough, φ might quite well be raised without any fall of consumption per employed worker. The raising of it might even be consistent with a rise in real wages, since we have abstracted not only from technical innovation, but also from other factors in changing productivity, such as organization, training, experience and 'social climate', and the possibility of acquiring temporarily supplies of consumer goods from outside our model—e.g. by an import surplus or by reduced consumption on the part of non-productive consumers.

It is tempting to use this effect of a changing φ as an explanation of the lower Soviet growth-rates in the '50s compared with those of the period of intensive industrialization in the '30s. During the earlier period there is no doubt that the value of φ was exceptionally high,* and by common admission (even by those who have 'deflated' the calculations expressed in 'constant prices of 1926–7') the growth-rate was quite exceptionally high. In the 1950s the value of φ is evidently lower; the growth-rates of the two sectors are much closer together; real wages have been rising sharply and the overall growth-rate has been lower than pre-war, possibly by nearly a third. A difficulty about this explanation is that one would have expected a high value of φ in the pre-war decade to have produced a rising rate of investment. But of this there is no sign after the initial stepping-up of this rate at the beginning of the First Five Year Plan: if anything the rate of investment seems to have fallen somewhat from the middle '30s onwards. This may possibly be a statistical illusion owing (as Domar points out) † to a faster rate of increase in productivity in the capital goods industries than in the economy as a whole, which would have the effect of reducing the value of I compared with Y when both were valued

* Cf. N. Kaplan, 'Soviet Capital Formation and Industrialization' (Rand Corporation, 1952; privately issued), pp. 37–9, 56–9; also in *Soviet Economic Growth*, ed. A. Bergson (Evanston, 1953), pp. 63–5, 78–80.

† *Essays in the Theory of Economic Growth* (New York, 1957), pp. 238–9.

at *current* prices. One has to remember, however, that a number of other relevant factors besides φ were changing at the same time—changes in agricultural productivity and in the terms of trade with agriculture (which in the U.S.S.R. constitutes a sector apart from the two industrial sectors of which we have been speaking), changes in technical knowledge and *expertise*, and following a period of rapid growth in the stock of capital equipment a catching-up of the replacement-demand upon sector 1 (which we have advisedly ignored), with a consequent absorption into replacement of a larger proportion of the gross investment-potential.

Having emphasized the fall in consumption per employed worker as the price of raising the growth-rate by raising φ, we should forthwith proceed to emphasize that this is not the same thing as a fall in total consumption, or even in consumption *per capita* of the population, if there has previously been an unemployed reserve. On the contrary, total consumption is bound to rise so long as any part at all of the investment is devoted to sector 2; and it is a misunderstanding to suppose that a rise in φ must entail a fall in consumption. The existing volume of consumption is, indeed, determined by the existing productive capacity of sector 2; it is thus the legacy of past history which cannot be modified in a retrograde direction unless there is actual *dis*investment in this sector. What is affected by the size of φ is the destination of *new additions* to productive capacity; thereby is decided whether expansion shall take place in sector 1 or sector 2. It is, of course, quite true that consumption in the near future will rise faster if φ is given a low value than if it has a high one. To this extent an expansion of consumption and a high growth-rate stand in conflict; just as we saw earlier, in connection with choice of technique, there can be a conflict between growth-rate and employment. What is often not appreciated is that this conflict applies only within a fairly narrow time-horizon, and disappears after a certain date, because the smaller share of a larger volume of investment may yield a larger growth of consumption, both absolutely and proportionately, than a larger share of a smaller total. Thus a development-path characterized by a high value of φ may so enlarge the output-capacity of sector 1 as to enable even the output of consumer goods to advance more rapidly than it could have done if a development-path with a lower value of φ had been taken—and this at a much earlier date than is commonly realized. (Of course in the limiting case where φ = 1, the conflict is absolute and for all time.)

In this connection one cannot refrain from quoting some illuminating calculations made by Professor Domar in his recently published *Essays.** For the purpose of these calculations he assumes, as we have done, that the capital-output ratio is the same in the two sectors, and adopts for it a value of 3. He assumes an initial rate of investment no higher than one tenth of the national income; and proceeds to plot consumption-curves for various values of our φ (which he writes as γ); with the initial level of consumption in Year o taken as equal to 9 (and national income or total net output as 10).

There are two boundary cases, (a) where φ = 1, (b) where φ = o. With (a) consumption never rises, since *no* part of investment is ever devoted to the consumer goods industries. With (b) the *whole* of what is invested (= the net output of the capital goods industries) goes into the consumer goods sector, and consumption is bound to rise faster in the early years than under any alternative policy. This is accordingly taken as a term of comparison, since it is to begin with the most favourable to consumption. Consumption will in this case rise by a given absolute amount each year; but the proportional rate of growth will be a declining one over time (when φ = o, it *must* be below the critical level as long as any net investment is occurring). By the ninth year consumption will have risen from its initial level of *9* to *12* and by the 18th year to *15*; but not until year 27 will the initial consumption-level be doubled.

With nearly all intermediate levels of φ, however, consumption will rise above the φ = o line not later than the 12th or 13th year, and thereafter rise more or less rapidly above it. For example, with the very high value of ·9 for φ consumption will scarcely rise at all for the first quinquennium and will remain substantially below the φ = o line for the whole of the first decade; but after the 12th year it will rise above it and by year 20 will have risen to some *4* times the initial level or more. With values for φ between ·2 and ·5 the consumption curve will rise above the φ = o line *within the first decade*, and by the end of

* *Ibid.,* pp. 248–50.

the second decade will have reached a level between double and treble the initial level.*

It seems worth emphasizing a corollary that was mentioned *en passant* at the start of this chapter: that in order to achieve a high growth-rate, it may be more important to give a high value to φ (i.e. a high investment-priority to the capital goods industries) than to have a large proportion of income invested initially. This could be expressed by saying that what you do with the current *increment* of national output is more important than whatever ratio of 'savings' to national income you happen to have inherited from the past (although legacies may contribute much towards easing present endeavour).† We have seen that a high value of φ will have the result of raising the average ratio of investment to total output as time goes on, and the average ratio will eventually catch up with the marginal ratio unless φ is raised further. But this rise in the average ratio will be quite consistent with rising total consumption, which can occur precisely because in the past a large proportion of the output of sector 1 has been ploughed-back to enlarge the investment-potential.

I would add to this corollary two general comments. Firstly, it seems possible that one of the reasons for the stagnation of underdeveloped countries and a crucial obstacle confronting any 'take-off' into industrialization may be the difficulty that such countries have in raising the coefficient φ above the 'critical level', low though in their situation this 'critical level' is likely to be. Even if temporarily raised, it is liable in face of various social and political pressures to relapse fairly quickly, and with it the proportional growth-rate. In a more developed country the obstacles to raising it may be less intractable, because the

* An interesting incidental result pointed out by Professor Domar is that the capital-output ratio of sector 1 has more influence than the value of his y (our φ), until y becomes very large, in determining the year in which the consumption-curve intersects the $y=0$ line. The size of the capital coefficient of sector 2 does not affect the result (*ibid.*, pp. 249–50).

† By virtue of what it terms a high "marginal rate of saving" (at first estimated at the high figure of 50 per cent) the Report on the Indian Second Five Year Plan estimated that the (average) rate of investment would rise from 7 per cent of the national income in 1955–6 to 11 per cent in 1960–1 and to 16 per cent in 1970–1 (Government of India Planning Commission, *Second Five Year Plan* (Delhi, 1956), p. 10). In the original Draft Recommendations of Professor P. C. Mahalanobis a quarter of all investment was to be in industry, and of this some two thirds in capital goods production.

standard of life is already higher. I am far from wishing to maintain that this is the only or even the main obstacle to advance in an underdeveloped country: more important, as we have seen, may well be the smallness of the agricultural surplus, or the 'waste' of it on relatively unproductive purposes, which sets a limit upon total investment; and to the extent that this is so, the removal of this bottleneck and the raising of φ may even stand in contradiction. (The need, for instance, to woo a peasant agriculture with offers of more industrial consumer goods in return for foodstuffs and raw materials may impose a priority in expansion for the consumer goods sector of industry.) The second comment that I am coming to is probably more relevant in most cases than absolute lowness of the wage-level as a reason why the traditional bias of development towards the path of 'textiles first' has proved to be so strong.* Nonetheless it may be *an* aspect of the tendency for the gap between poor countries and rich countries to get wider.

My second comment is that a development path characterized by a high (even a moderately high) value of φ is a very improbable one for a capitalist economy to pursue (with the possible exception of short bursts of Schumpeterian optimism on the part of particular *entrepreneurs*, such as those that engaged in the railroad-race to the Pacific Coast in North America in the 1860s, or heavy industry development prompted by war). The reason for this improbability is that such a development-path implies, *par excellence*, an investment in increased productive capacity in the capital goods industries *in advance* of any foreseeable expansion in the market for them. It is, indeed, the outstanding example of what we have called the Accelerator-in-Reverse, since it represents an expansion of capital goods production in order thereby to promote an expansion of sector-2 capacity and hence of consumption at subsequent dates; the causal process moving in the opposite direction from the one with which a capitalist economy is familiar. Hence this type of

---

* Cf. the remark of Professor W. Rostow: "The development of a cotton-textile industry sufficient to meet domestic requirements has not generally imparted a sufficient impulse in itself to launch a self-sustaining growth process." Railway building in the past, he thinks, was far more important. However, his search for an explanation is predominantly in terms of the effect on *demand* occasioned by the growth of some 'leading sector'. ('The Take-Off into Self-Sustained Growth' in *Economic Journal*, March 1956, p. 44.)

development is particularly subject to those obstacles to growth in an unplanned economy of which we spoke in Chapter I. Indeed it implies for a whole period an expansion of capacity in these industries solely to meet the needs of future investment programmes in sector 1 itself—investment undertaken in the belief that investment will continue at the same rate and in roughly the same form, as an outlet for the products of the increased capacity that this investment process is creating. Moreover, increasingly high rates of investment have to be maintained as development proceeds. In a planless economy ruled by the market individual *entrepreneurs* can have no assurance that such a level of investment in expanding the capital goods sector will continue. Any expectation that it will do so can only be an act of faith—a triumph of irrationality in a system that economists and economic historians claim has exalted rationality to be the sovereign rule of business life! If such an expectation should chance to be entertained for a time, it must inevitably be most delicately poised and liable to be thrown off balance by the merest puff of rumour or changing mood. Such a course could only be a rational procedure for long if it were set within the framework of a development plan that linked present programmes with the perspective of some kind of trend and pattern of development projected into the future. That this is so may be the reason why so little attention has been paid to a structural pattern of this type in the discussion of rival growth-models, and why if mentioned at all it has been dismissed (at any rate until quite recently) as impossibly heterodox.

VI

PRICE-RELATIONS

THE kind of structural relationships that we have been discussing will evidently be the main preoccupation of any
planned economy because they are relationships crucial for
growth. They are not such as the market is at all well qualified
to look after. In so far as they are concerned with events separated in time, and require both vision and deliberation if they
are to be anything but accidental, the market can yield no
guidance at all. In the long period (which may not be so long
as to be disregarded even by the shortsighted) correct decisions
about such relationships may contribute much more to human
welfare than could the most perfect micro-economic adjustment,
of which the market (if it worked like the textbooks, at least,
and there were no income-inequalities) is admittedly more fitted
in most cases to take care. In so far as a choice has to be made
between the two, there can scarcely be reasonable doubt as to
which one should choose; and while there seems to be no general
reason why a planned economy should not look after the micro-
economic adjustments well enough together with the macro-,
there may be particular reasons why attention to the one conflicts with or detracts from the other.* A good strategic plan
combined with good tactics in its execution is no doubt the

* Cf. the opinion of Mr. Peter Wiles that "too delicate a comprehension of
'scarcity' problems, a determination never to violate Professor Lerner's welfare
equations for however short a period or in however unimportant a connection,
slows up the rate of growth ... balance means investing at the pace of the slowest.
... Growth conflicts at certain points with consumers' sovereignty and even with
'scarcity' itself." ('Growth versus Choice' in *Economic Journal*, June 1956, pp. 248–9,
251.)

military ideal; what seemed an invincible strategy may sometimes be frustrated by bad tactics; but if strategy is lacking,
tactics can evidently have very little chance.

As regards price-relations (with which so far we have not been
concerned) it is clear that there are two major ones that are
closely connected with growth. These can be spoken of as
macro-relations in that they are relations not between the prices
of individual commodities but between the price-*levels* of aggre-
gates. Firstly, there is the relation between wages (as the price-
level, or structure of prices, of labour) and the price-level of
capital goods. Secondly, there is that between wages and the
retail price-level of consumer goods. The second of these will
define the level of real wages; and the first will influence the
choice of technique (in so far as this is affected by prices at all)
by defining the cost of substituting capital goods for labour in
production, or alternatively of getting additional output by
using more direct labour rather than installing machinery or
using more fuel and power and materials (if these proportions
can be varied). To the question of these two crucial macro-
price-relations we shall return in the second half of the chapter.

It is the belief that the demands of growth and of micro-
economic adjustment stand in conflict that has manifestly influenced those who in the discussions of the last few years in the
planned economies of eastern Europe have resisted measures of
decentralization which smacked of 'market autonomism' and
seemed in danger of weakening the capacity for central co-
ordination and steering of development. In the first stage of
development in these countries, when the paramount need was
for a break with traditional economic patterns, for large structural shifts and a rapid build-up of a growth-potential in the
basic power and metal and machine-making industries, this
argument had great force and was most likely to go unques-
tioned. There were even some ready to assert that planning need
pay no attention at all to the market, or to indices derived
therefrom, apart from ensuring that retail prices were so adjusted relatively to demand as to prevent damaging forms of
disequilibrium in the retail market (such as acute shop-shortages
and queues)—a necessity imposed by the existence of 'two forms
of socialist property', with its corollary of trading relations between town and country, and by the use of wage-differentials as

a production-incentive during the 'first period of socialism'. In other words, they were unwilling to contemplate the market as 'influencing' production at all, let alone 'regulating' it, which would have been the negation of planning. As for the transfer-prices at which goods passed from one State enterprise to another *within* the State sector, these seem to have been treated in the main as having an arbitrary character and not subscribing to any general rule. While it was recognized that in the interests of efficiency such prices must be related to 'planned costs', the notion prevailed apparently that they could be treated solely as planning instruments, wielded *ad hoc* so as to promote the objectives of the Plan but not reciprocally influencing planning calculations and decisions.*

It is this standpoint, with its denial of the possibility of any compromise between centralized planning and the market, that has been questioned in the discussions of the last few years, notably in Poland but also in the Soviet Union and to a less extent in East Germany as well. Discussion was doubtless given some impetus in this direction by the statement (more forthright than anything previously said on the subject, though still quite abstract) in Stalin's *Economic Problems of Socialism in the U.S.S.R.*† that in the market for consumer goods "the law of value preserves, within certain limits, the function of a regulator", and that its operation "is not confined to the sphere of commodity circulation" but "also extends to production". Here, while it "has no regulating function", "it nevertheless influences production, and this fact cannot be ignored when directing production". But to a large extent discussion of such matters can be regarded as a sequel to the debate about indices for comparing alternative investment projects to which we have

---

* The rigour of this attitude was modified a little after a well-known pronouncement in 1943, which stated *inter alia* that the law of value still "functions under socialism", although no longer "as an elemental law of the market" but "in a transformed manner" ('Some Questions on the Teaching of Political Economy' in *Pod Znamenem Marksizma*, 1943, no. 7–8; published in trans. in *American Economic Review*, Sept. 1944, p. 501 *seq.*). However, although this was acknowledged in general terms (often in the generalization, meaningless *per se*, that "the total of prices must equal the total of values"), emphasis was simultaneously laid on the fact that "price and value do not and cannot coincide in the case of separate commodities", and that their very divergence was used to further the aims of socialist planning (N. Voznesensky, *War Economy in the U.S.S.R.* (Moscow, 1948), p. 117. For a summary of the discussion up to 1956 cf. R. L. Meek, *Studies in the Labour Theory of Value*, pp. 256–84). † Moscow, 1952, p. 23.

alluded earlier and which arose from the practical needs of planning and project-making. Although such indices were conceived purely as planning instruments for internal use in Gosplan or at the Ministerial level, their application in any concrete setting immediately raised the question of the economic significance of the prices in which these indices were expressed. If these prices were arbitrary ones, how much could the indices tell one? (This, as we have seen, was in effect Strumilin's line of criticism of the 'coefficient of effectiveness' as customarily used.)

This new post-1953 debate concentrated on three main issues.* Firstly, there was the question of the proper relationship between the price-level of capital goods (including all intermediate products exchanged between State enterprises) and the retail price-level of consumer goods: whether the former was too low relatively to the latter (thereby *inter alia* encouraging uneconomic use of capital goods) and the two price-levels should be brought into a uniform relation with one another.† Secondly, there was the question of whether, if there were to be a reform of prices *within* each sector, the guiding principle should be 'values' (in the Marxian sense) or 'prices of production'. Advocates of the latter urged in effect that otherwise the criterion for the comparative effectiveness of investment as *between* different industries would be adversely affected. Thirdly, there was the question of whether the prices of capital goods should continue to be 'planned prices', constructed on the basis of (planned) cost, or whether they should be allowed to vary so as in some way (not very clearly defined) to reflect differences or variations in the prices of consumer goods (which, so far as retail prices were concerned, admittedly bore the character of supply-demand 'market prices').‡

The relevance of all this to our present theme is that it marks a shift of preoccupation towards questions of micro-economic adjustment and the relation of these to a market mechanism—

* Apart from the more abstract question of whether the influence of the law of value under socialism depends basically on the existence of 'two forms of socialist property' or on the 'character of social labour' and hence of the wage-system under socialism (payment according to work).

† This was the view advanced by Kronrod and also by Strumilin.

‡ The latter was proposed by Professor W. Brus in Poland; it happens in Yugoslavia where there exist markets for capital goods; but in the Soviet discussion it seems to have found no advocates.

nothing like a complete shift, of course, but nonetheless a genuine attempt to find some *modus vivendi* between planning and market, between care for the macro-relations of socialist development and for micro-adjustments, especially within the consumer goods sector, between rapid growth and giving consumers the 'assortment' of goods they desire. It can scarcely be by chance that this shift of emphasis came at a stage of development when economic backwardness had been left behind, when priority for capital goods production, though maintained and reaffirmed as a cardinal principle, had been greatly eased, when consumption standards in consequence were rising fast and official pronouncements had come to speak about catching-up during the next decade and a half the consumption standards of the older industrial countries of the West. It was quite clear that the previous system, despite remarkable achievements in growth, had involved considerable waste (waste that was probably large in absolute terms although small relatively to the growth achieved), and had become so overcentralized as to render control by the centre over much of the detail of what was planned more nominal than real. Professor Oskar Lange has likened the situation to what tends to happen in any war economy.* The result was that the *de facto* discretion of enterprises was considerable, and this commonly took the form of various clandestine decentralized arrangements between them (e.g. the role of the *tolkachi*). A recurrent complaint of Gosplan was the tendency to fulfil output plans at the expense of quality, and the failure to fulfil the 'assortment plans' (i.e. the range of types or varieties of a product); enterprises tending to concentrate on those types that were most easily produced, or contributed most to the quantitative output-target according to the magnitude in terms of which this was calculated, or alternatively showed the largest profit-margin at existing prices.

On both sides there were those who were strongly sceptical of the possibility of any such *modus vivendi* between planning and the market. Centralizers believed that any substantial conces-

---

* He considers that "if not totally then at least in large measure, there was an element of historical necessity" for this centralized system; although such methods "which replaced economic stimuli with administrative decisions", while "necessary and beneficial during a certain period, cannot be permanent methods for administering the national economy". (*Some Problems Relating to the Polish Road to Socialism*, Warsaw, 1957, p. 13.)

sion to market influences would progressively loosen planned control until the pendulum swung back to complete 'market autonomism', with its cumulative tendencies and its absence oɪ *ex ante* co-ordination. Even such macro-price relationships as those to which we referred earlier in this chapter would become subject to the market and hence stand in conflict with the growth-requirements of the plan. On the other hand, decentralizers and admirers of the competitive ideal (more numerous doubtless in the west than in the east) agreed with them to the extent of thinking that no compromise-position could yield prices that were objectively-based and hence economically significant unless they were completely subject to market influences; and until they were, micro-adjustments would continue to be defective. Here is not the place to traverse again this old debate. But three observations are perhaps admissible about the conditions that it would seem necessary for any compromise (or should one say 'coexistence'?) between planning and market to fulfil.

Firstly, it seems clear that the keystone of any such compromise must be a system of economic incentives to the enterprise. These incentives would need to be so devised that what is profitable for the enterprise to do coincides with (or at least does not seriously conflict with) what is socially desirable in the light of the general objectives of the plan, while at the same time having some relation to the market. We have seen that under the most centralized system a good deal of *de facto* discretion must inevitably rest with the management of an enterprise. At any rate, inventiveness as well as co-operation will only be forthcoming if there is sufficient inducement to show initiative, and to show it in the right direction and not in a wrong one. In U.S.S.R. and eastern Europe during the past period bonuses for plan fulfilment apparently submerged the influence of the earlier payments into the so-called Director's Fund out of excess profits (which was discontinued entirely during the war period but later restored under the name of the Enterprise Fund). Sometimes they conflicted; and often when the target was defined in terms of gross output the plan-fulfilment bonuses encouraged concentration on the production of things with a high raw

material content and low value-added.* Recently, however,
there has been a restoration of payments out of profit to pride
of place (either as bonuses or for purposes, such as housing or
club-facilities, beneficial to members of the enterprise), not only
in Poland, Czechoslovakia and Hungary but, in some degree
also it would seem, in the U.S.S.R. In Yugoslavia, where the
'autonomy of the enterprise' is carried to an extreme and enterprises can buy and sell freely and even fix their own prices, the
whole 'net income of the enterprise' after payment of a basic
wage is at the disposal of the enterprise (either for investment or
for distribution as an earnings-supplement among its members).
It is fairly clear that, *provided* the selling price is pre-fixed, incentive based on profitability is most calculated to encourage
efficiency in the sense of cost-reduction; and profitability is
bound to influence an enterprise in some degree (if it retains any
part of the profit it earns), even when there are bonuses based
on other criteria. It does not necessarily follow, however, that
this will encourage the most desirable or most economical output-pattern—whether it does so will depend on the pattern of
prices in terms of which profitability is calculated.

We must accordingly have as our second condition that the
structure of prices is such as to cause incentives to operate in the
proper way; and the more that incentives at the enterprise-level
are geared to profitability, and the more extensive the economic
decisions that are influenced by them, the more important does
this question of prices become. In varying degrees the enterprise may have a say in matters of investment policy;† and

---

* Cf. A. Nove in *Economica*, 1958, p. 1; esp. the example of why it was difficult
to get spare parts for tractors; also R. W. Davies, *The Development of the Soviet
Budgetary System*, Cambridge 1958, p. 324, esp. the example of the effect on bed-
stead design when the plan-target was defined in terms of weight; and R. Janakieff,
'Critical Comments on the use of the Gross Production Index', trans. in *International
Economic Papers*, no. 8, esp. pp. 184–7, who (on the basis of Bulgarian and East
German experience) condemns this index, *inter alia*, for the bias it creates towards
material-intensive products. The 'New Economic Model' adopted by the State
Economic Council in Poland in 1957 proposed terminating both the use of gross
output as an index of plan-fulfilment and also the linking of economic incentives
with indices of plan-fulfilment.

† In the U.S.S.R. there has been a slight lifting of the ceiling upon 'small investments' which an enterprise can decide for itself; in Poland the percentage of all
investments decentralized to the enterprise-level is now between a fifth and a third;
in Yugoslavia and also apparently in Czechoslovakia it is even higher than this
(see *Economic Survey of Europe for 1957*, U.N.E.C.E., Geneva 1958, chap. i, p 39).

current repair and maintenance of plant is certainly within their competence, *de facto* if not *de jure*. If prices of capital goods are too high, this will create a bias against technical innovation and labour-saving; if they are too low, this will encourage wasteful use of machinery and inattention to repairs and upkeep; just as too low prices for fuel and power or raw materials will discourage fuel economy or saving in raw material. If catering for quality and variety can make no difference to the selling-price per unit, there will be a bias towards concentrating entirely on long runs of a few standardized products and those of cheapest input-content.

When it comes, however, to laying down pricing-rules, matters are less obvious. In discussing this it is as well to speak separately about the two main sectors, and convenient to make the usual distinction between long- and short-period decisions, even though these may shade off into one another.

Let us take first the consumer goods sector. One way of providing a priority-index for investment decisions, governing rates of expansion of productive capacity in different industries, would be to calculate in each case the ratio of the retail price (which is a real market price in normal circumstances) to cost price, and to multiply this by the additional output-capacity (e.g. per annum) that the expenditure of a given amount of investment would create.* This is roughly equivalent to multiplying the output-capacity-creating effect of a given amount of investment in a particular line of production by the appropriate rate of turnover tax (or mark-up between the factory selling-price and the retail price-less-distributive-costs). Alternatively a 'normal price' could be calculated for each product (as a purely accounting price for planning purposes), to include some standard rate of profit or of turnover tax (uniformly related to amount of capital employed) added on to its cost price as calculated at the factory level. Investment-priority would then be given to increasing the output of those goods with the highest ratio of retail price to 'normal price'.†

---

* To allow for differences in the expected life of different plants or pieces of equipment, it would be necessary to include an appropriate amortization-charge, calculated on a per-unit-of-output basis, in the cost price of output.

† Cf. an article by the present writer in *Gospodarka Planowa*, Warsaw 1956, no. 10. (Cf. Oskar Lange, *The Political Economy of Socialism*, Netherlands School of Economics, Rotterdam 1958, p. 27.)

In so far as short-term decisions, especially regarding quality and assortment, are affected by what is profitable to the enterprise, there may be something to be said for making the selling prices that enterprises receive for their products (the Russian *optovie tseni*, but *sans* turnover tax) stand in some relationship to the retail prices of these products. Since the latter express the supply-demand situation *vis-a-vis* consumers, this would enable differences in the current supply-demand situation of different goods to be reflected in the prices paid to the enterprises, and so provide an inducement for enterprises to concentrate upon producing things that are in shortest supply. The quite serious difficulty about this device, if at all liberally employed, is that it would conflict with the use of selling price (e.g. when based upon planned cost *plus* a conventional margin) as an efficiency lever to encourage cost-reduction through economy of input. In so far as selling prices were aligned with market price instead of cost in order to make the output of some things more profitable to the enterprise than others, these more profitable things would be more easily produced and the pressure to cost-reduction in their case would to this extent be lessened.

An alternative to adjusting factory selling price to market price would be to rely on orders transmitted from a wholesale organization, so far as short-period variation in the output-pattern is concerned.* The wholesale organization will presumably base its orders to the producing enterprise on the stock-turnover of various lines at the retail stage. A disadvantage of relying upon this as an indicator of demand is that in a chronic state of short supply the consumer may have to be content with buying what is available, whether preferred or second-best, and there need be nothing to tell the wholesale

---

* This seems to have been the method generally relied upon hitherto in the planned economies. In Poland, except for certain basic products, the plan will now prescribe only the net value of output for an enterprise, but not the detailed assortment. In Roumania it has recently been enacted that consumer goods enterprises may modify their output plans in agreement with trading enterprises. In U.S.S.R. there are listed products for which the enterprise can change its assortment plan by agreement with the buying organization. In Hungary selling prices paid to enterprises in the consumer goods sector, which previously yielded quite arbitrary differences in the profit-margin on different things, have been revised so as to yield uniform profit-margins, with the object of giving more influence to the demand transmitted through trading organs. Exceptionally, however, in cases of special shortage the profit-margin is deliberately widened to encourage an increase of supply.

organization which is the consumers' first choice and which his
aute de mieux. In a different state of the retail market, however,
where the general balance of supply and demand gives the
initiative to the consumer, stocks on the shelves rather than
queues having the tendency to lengthen, this objection loses
its force; and the rates of stock-turnover of different goods,
transmitted to the factory in different volumes of orders, might
suffice to ensure that the product-assortment matched consumers' demand. But for this purpose, retail prices would need
to be kept stable at some 'normal' price, instead of being
adjusted to demand.

To relate differences in factory selling price to differences in
market price would not necessarily mean to make the two sets of
prices *equal* (even after deducting distributive costs from the
latter). The disadvantage of making them equal would be that
to do so would make the profit accruing to the enterprise unduly
large (for reasons we shall mention in a moment). Unless enterprises were to be responsible, in decentralized fashion, for both
deciding and financing all industrial investment, this would
have little point, and would indeed leave enterprises too rich
and easy-going as well as so financially independent as to be
immune to financial controls. It would be 'featherbedding' of
the enterprises. To avoid this, the bulk of the profits would have
to be taxed in some way into the Budget; leaving the residual
position much the same* as though the two sets of prices (retail
and factory selling) were different and the gap bridged by a
turnover tax or excise.

What has been suggested for the consumer goods sector would
lose much of its point, however, unless the prices of input were
constructed on some consistent principle; since these would
enter into the standard 'normal prices' suggested above as well
as into the actual factory selling prices of consumer goods. From
the standpoint of the enterprises using these inputs it might
seem that only the price-relationship of inputs that are directly
substitutable really matter. It is true that in such cases the price-
ratios matter a good deal more, since these ratios will help to
determine which of the alternatives are most used and which are

* With an important qualification, however, that is mentioned below, pp. 95–7.

economized upon. But inputs are always substitutable *indirectly* to the extent that the products into which they enter can be substituted for one another or turned out in varying proportions; and for purposes of accounting prices used by the planning or projecting authorities in their calculations uniformity of principle in constructing prices of inputs must manifestly extend over the whole range. What is crucial here is the relationship between the prices of mechanical equipment and the level of wages, since there is always some range over which mechanical equipment and human labour are substitutable even in the short run (e.g. the usage of machinery and its upkeep). But analogous considerations apply to the prices of raw materials and of fuel and power relatively to one another and to the labour that is using them.

We come, accordingly, to the first of those macro-price relations of which we have already spoken and with which the last of our three observations about the price-structure is concerned. We do so because the question of what is the 'correct' relationship between the price-level of capital goods and of 'living labour' enters into the determination not only of the *general* level but also of the structure of *relative prices* of capital goods. It enters into both aspects for the simple reason that capital goods involve capital goods in their own production and in various proportions (also different turnover periods of the labour and resources invested or 'stored up' in them). Hence one cannot know how the structure of *relative* prices of products of this sector is to be determined until one has answered the more general question.

Clearly if labour productivity is constant* the question of what is to be the relationship between the general *level* of prices of capital goods (or alternatively of the price of some representative or standard product of this sector) and wages as the price of 'living labour' is the same as the question of what *agio*, or 'mark-up', to include in the price of capital goods over and above their own cost in wages paid for the labour directly or indirectly employed in their production. From what was said above in Chapter II it would appear that there is no way of

* If productivity changes, then the price of a machine may change relatively to that of a unit of labour even though the ratio of the price of a machine to its wage-cost remains constant (i.e. with a given proportional *agio*). See below, p. 94.

determining *a priori* what ideally this *agio* or premium should be, and of using it to determine the rate of investment and the choice of technique. But because it cannot be determined *a priori*, we do not have to conclude that it is not necessary or that it cannot be derived empirically in any given situation once certain key decisions about investment have been taken. It will be *a posteriori*, however, to these decisions and not *a priori*.

The reason why such an *agio* is necessary can be expressed quite simply in this way: namely that without it the demand for capital goods would always tend to exceed the available supply, so long as there remained any scope for raising the productivity of labour by installing new technical equipment and to the extent that there was any scope at all for enterprises (or some higher authority) to decide upon the amount and type of capital goods to purchase on the basis of their prices. If a machine (of any type) requiring x man-hours of labour to produce were to cost no more than the wages of x man-hours of labour, there would always be a tendency to install that machine in preference to the employment of that quantity of 'living labour' so long as the effect on production* of installing the machine exceeded the effect of employing x man-hours of labour directly. This substitution of 'stored-up labour' for 'living' would tend to occur in two main ways: by installing more costly equipment so long as this was more productive, and by reducing the degree of 'manning' of machinery with labour (including the amount of labour spent on upkeep and repair), so far as the proportions were variable in which labour and machinery could be combined. Thus there would be a chronic state of goods-shortage in the capital goods sector, just as there would be in the consumer goods sector if retail prices were not fixed at the requisite level about which we shall speak presently. True, the supply of capital goods at any one time is governed by the productive capacity of this sector, and this supply is capable of being enlarged by devoting more investment to an enlargement of productive capacity. But so long as there is any limit upon the investment potential of the economy (such as we have discussed in previous chapters), this sector cannot be enlarged indefin-

---

* This effect in augmenting production would have to be summed over the expected life of the machine, or alternatively both its cost *and* its productive effect reduced to an annual basis.

itely; and until all technical needs are sated, the state of goods-shortage, or of excess demand, will continue.*

Once the investment policy, in its main essentials, has been defined in the plan, it should be possible to arrive at this *agio* as a 'trial and error' rate of premium to be entered uniformly in the price of all capital goods. Investment policy as defined in the plan would presumably stipulate the general volume of investment (depending on the existing output-capacity of the capital goods sector), its rate of increase (or the amount of current investment to be devoted to enlarging this sector), and also in general outline the technical form of investment (e.g. by setting a general coefficient of effectiveness or by stipulating the standard type of construction-project to be adopted in each of the main industries). It would be necessary to find empirically a price-level of capital goods that brought the demand for them from all sources into balance with the given supply of such goods.

At first sight it might seem as though such a balance could be achieved equally well by adjusting the investment funds made available *via* the plan to industry. True, the overall demand could be influenced in this way and could be set at any level; and according to the level that was set the price-level of capital goods would have to be adjusted appropriately. In so far, however, as any discretion was left to enterprises to adapt or to supplement investment plans from their own resources (or from bank credit)—and we have seen that in matters of current maintenance and replacement such discretion is bound to exist *de facto*—the demand for capital goods could not be controlled completely by controlling financial allocations. More important, control over the *general* level of demand would still leave open the possibility of shifts in demand between different *types* of capital goods. This is where the structure of relative prices within sector 1 becomes relevant. In short, the *agio*, or rate of

* Cf. V. V. Novozhilov, 'On Choosing between Investment Projects', trans. in *International Economic Papers*, no. 6, p. 7: "The production of all reproducible means of production is restricted by the limited volume of investment in the economy (investment is limited, not in the sense that it is absolutely small, but that it is less than the volume of effective investment opportunities). . . . No branch of the economy escapes this relation . . . everywhere expenditure of these means rests on the same general limitation—the limit to the amount of investment in the economy as a whole." This gives rise to what he calls "inversely related costs" of any investment project.

premium, would have to be such as to adjust the relative prices of different capital goods (produced under various conditions as regards the employment of capital goods in their own production) so as to make it worth-while for enterprises to adopt that choice of technique that the plan intended (or which maximized growth). This condition as well as the former one (concerning the overall balance) would have to be fulfilled. The adjustment of prices in this manner would help to ensure that the capital goods available were used to best advantage and to discourage their wasteful use.

To avoid possible misunderstanding, it should be mentioned that the inclusion of such a premium or 'mark up' in the transfer prices of capital goods would not necessarily involve its inclusion in the price *paid* to the producing enterprise. The difference could be bridged by an appropriate rate of turnover tax (whether this is the best device to adopt is a matter to which we shall return). Ideally, however, such a tax would need to be related to the capital involved in the production of the good in question (to allow for differences in amount and in the period of turnover of this capital) and not to its prime cost: i.e. it would need to be levied at a uniform proportional rate in relation to the former.*

There is, it is true, an obvious defect in relying on this empirical (trial and error) method of determining the supplement to be included in the selling price of capital goods: namely, that

---

* An alternative method would be, of course, to make an interest charge for all installed capital equipment (and also for funds of circulating capital). This charge would then be automatically included in an enterprise's costs (as it would also be, presumably, in the cost on which 'accounting prices' were based). In Yugoslavia there is a tax on enterprises proportioned to their fixed capital. According to the new Polish Economic Model centrally controlled investments, though non-repayable, carry an interest-charge to the enterprise; and 'supplementary investments' made by enterprises can be financed by repayable credits which also carry an interest-charge. Among the recommendations of the Theses for the New Economic Model the following statement appears: "From the standpoint of economy of durable and expensive resources as a whole as well as of a correct cost and price calculation the question of paying interest on the entire capital made available to the enterprises should be considered." Yet another possibility is a suggestion made by Professor Bronislaw Minc that turnover tax should be made equi-proportional to the wage-fund weighted by some index of the "technical equipment of labour", e.g. the amortisation quota (*Voprosi Ekonomiki*, 1958, no. 1, p. 96). As we shall see below, however, such methods, aimed at adjusting the relative costs of different capital goods, are probably insufficient *per se* to secure an optimum choice of technique.

the result would largely depend on how far, and with what degree of strictness, capital goods were allocated by the plan between industries and between enterprises. It is scarcely possible to separate planning of total investment from the planning of particular investment projects (at least the larger ones) composing that total. If total investment at any one time is determined by the output capacity of this sector, so will this be true of particular categories of capital goods and hence of particular types of investment project using these different categories. It might seem, therefore, that there could be no uniform *agio* introduced into the prices of *all* types of capital goods: that this *agio* would have to vary with the particular scarcities (in relation to the current demand for them) of particular types. This is, indeed, the case for permitting sector 1 prices *as well as* those of sector 2 to vary with the demand (including the demand emanating from the market for consumer goods). We have to remember that in this, more practical, context capital goods include not only machinery but also raw materials and semi-finished components (where these pass hands between enterprises)—not only 'instruments of labour' but also 'objects of labour'—and the same pricing-rules may not be appropriate for both. There may well be certain things in sufficiently scarce supply, especially scarce materials or fuels (oil has been an example in the past), to require the inclusion of an abnormally high rate of turnover tax in their transfer-prices in order to restrict their use.

On the other hand, there are some strong reasons for treating such cases as exceptional and stabilizing the prices of capital goods so far as possible according to some long-term principle uniformly applied. The main reason is that, in so far as capital goods enter into the costs of industries using them and thereby affect their investment decisions, short-term fluctuations in their prices, such as would result from adjusting these prices to particular scarcities, would tend to cause decisions about technique, location, etc., to be made that from a long-term standpoint were wrong decisions. To avoid this, it might be preferable for the method of planned allocations of capital goods to be employed to handle particular scarcities, rather than the method of short-period price-adjustments.

What then of the second of our two macro-price relations,

that between wages and the (retail) price-level of consumer goods; or what comes to much the same thing, the relation between the level of industrial cost-price and the (retail) price-level of consumer goods? Incidental to this question is that of the relation between the price-levels of the two sectors, producing respectively consumer goods and capital goods.

It is now a sufficiently familiar principle* that the difference between the retail price of consumer goods and the cost at which they are produced (when these costs are reckoned at the wages paid out at all stages of production back to raw materials and including the wage-cost of amortisation of equipment) will be dependent largely (though not exclusively) upon the rate of investment, and will vary with the latter. This is equivalent to saying that, with a given level of productivity, the relation between money wages and the price-level of consumer goods will be a function of the rate of growth of the economy: a proposition that looks closely akin to what has been said in previous chapters about the connection between wages and growth (although in our two models the causal relation was presented as being in opposite directions). It is indeed the monetary expression of those relations of our earlier models, and it acquires importance from the fact that the retail market is a market in the full sense even in a socialist economy. This simple but crucial postulate follows, of course, from the income-expenditure balance about which we spoke in Chapter I, and seems to be the chief corollary that this type of approach to questions of growth has to offer to a planned economy. The reason is the very simple one that if there is to be equilibrium in the retail market,† and if no part of wages is saved, the total value of sales on the retail market must equal in any period the total wage-bills of sector 1 and

* Among the first to enunciate this principle (as applied to *total* profit, however, rather than to profit as a ratio) was, I believe, Professor M. Kalecki (cf. his *Essays in the Theory of Economic Fluctuations*, London, 1938, pp. 76–7), although something fairly similar was implied in a little-known work by Dr. E. C. Van Dorp, *A Simple Theory of Capital, Wages and Profit or Loss*, London, 1937, esp. pp. 83, 103. More recently it has been developed as a theory of distribution by Mr. N. Kaldor in the *Review of Economic Studies*, vol. xxiii, no. 2, pp. 94–6, and by Mrs. J. Robinson in *Accumulation of Capital*, London, 1956, pp. 74–5. For its application to a socialist economy cf. the present writer's *Political Economy and Capitalism*, London 1937, pp. 325–7, and 'Saving and Investment in a Socialist Economy' in the *Economic Journal*, Dec. 1939, p. 716.

† Including in the conditions of equilibrium not merely the absence of queues but also the absence of abnormal depletion or accumulation of stocks at any stage.

sector 2, whereas the prime cost of current output will consist
only of the wage-bill of sector 2 (*plus* any current expenditure
on purchases from sector 1 for maintenance and replacement
purposes). Only in conditions of zero net investment, when no
one is employed in sector 1 except on replacement work for itself
and for sector 2, will the difference, or margin, between the two
sets of prices disappear. *

It is perhaps of some interest to note that this principle, even
if it is a familiar one today, conflicts with what has apparently
been treated as an accepted corollary of older theories. This may
not be surprising since the former acquires its importance under
dynamic conditions, whereas the latter were theories of static
equilibrium. But there seems no good reason for supposing the
latter to apply even to stationary conditions. The corollary in
question, which has been held to follow from the theory of
marginal productivity, is that the profit or surplus above wages,
irrespective of how it is used, must be determined in a socialist
economy as in a capitalist one by the marginal productivity of
capital. † This seems to rest on a confusion between the determinants of the first and the second of our two macro-price
relations and in particular on a misconception about the latter.
We have just seen that (with any given level of productivity)
the relation between the price-level of consumer goods and
wages is dependent upon the growth-rate of the economy, and
in stationary conditions wages would necessarily absorb the
whole net product. ‡

If we depart from our simplified two-sector model and allow
for the existence of non-productive workers as income-receivers
and consumers, then we can say that the difference between the
retail price-level and costs must equal net investment *plus* these

* This is on the assumption that amortisation is included in the cost of consumer
goods and that charges for amortisation equal current expenditure on replacement.

† Cf. Professor Sir D. H. Robertson, *op. cit.*, p. 92. Professor Robertson remarks
that Cassel, "in his anxiety to prove the 'necessity' of interest", was misleading in
his statement (*Nature and Necessity of Interest*, p. 178) that the rate of interest must
be equal to the rate at which the stock of capital is increasing, in order to 'finance'
this increase. Cassel was not very explicit about his reason for this contention. Yet,
is it not possible that he had an inkling of the true relationship (if 'profit' bears the
same relation to national income as does investment, it will also bear the same
relation to existing capital as does investment)?

‡ Any profit over wages (or revenue from a turnover tax) in the case of capital
goods produced to meet current maintenance and replacement would in this
situation need to be used to subsidize the sale of consumer goods below cost.

other income payments that do not enter into the wage-bill (and hence costs) of our two industrial sectors. In Academician Strumilin's contribution to the Soviet discussion these other income payments were referred to as 'social consumption', and these together with investment expenditure as the 'surplus product' of society.* This 'surplus product' must accrue to industry in the form of profit, unless it is diverted directly into the State Budget before it reaches the enterprise by means of an excise duty or turnover tax. Thus the receipts from this tax *plus* profits tax should balance State expenditure on new investment *plus* 'social consumption'.† We can allow for this, and also for the fact that some part of personal incomes is saved or paid in direct taxes, by expanding the simplified formula $S = xLw$ (where S is the total profit or surplus product accruing in one form or another to the State, x stands for the ratio $L_i/(L_i + L_e)$ and $L = L_i + L_e$, to use the notation of our first model in Chapter III) into:

$$S = (x+y)Lw - (s+t)(Lw + yLw)$$

where y is the ratio of non-productive (in the sense of being employed outside either of our two production-sectors) to productive workers, and s and t represent the average proportions of wages and salaries that are respectively saved and taxed directly.

In so far as agriculture is not included in either of our two industrial sectors, and economic relations between them and agriculture represent an exchange of one kind of consumer goods for another (e.g. textiles for food), the size of this exchange need not affect our price-relationship, provided that the trade is a balanced trade. But to the extent that it represents an exchange of capital goods (e.g. agricultural machinery or fertilizers) against foodstuffs, it will be equivalent to an import surplus of consumer goods and will to that extent lower the ratio of retail prices to cost.

* *Voprosi Ekonomiki*, 1956, no. 12, pp. 96–100; *Planovoe Khoziaistvo*, 1957, no. 2, p. 38 *seq*. These other incomes included those of workers in the health, educational and defence services and in research and also of administrative workers above the level of industrial and trading enterprises.

† Cf. the present writer's *Soviet Economic Development since 1917*, London 1948, pp. 363–4.

When we come to the question of the relative price-levels of the two sectors, a distinction needs to be emphasized which hitherto we have chosen to ignore. In speaking of the relation between wages and the price of a unit of output one can take wages to refer either to any unit of labour arbitrarily defined or to whatever quantity of labour is embodied in a unit of output—to the wages of a man-hour (or man-day) or to the wage-*cost* of output. So long as the productivity of labour does not change, these two ratios will move in step with one another, and given the productivity either ratio is derivative from the other. But when productivity changes this will no longer be the case. Clearly it is the second of the two definitions that is relevant to any talk about 'uniformity' or 'non-uniformity' of sector price-levels.

If there were a market in the full sense for capital goods as there is for consumer goods, and if in addition investment were financed out of the profits of enterprises (or from repayable credits) at the discretion of enterprises, without any effective planning of the distribution of such investment between the sectors, there would have to be a uniform price-level for both sectors: a uniform price-level, i.e., in the sense that prices were constructed in both cases on the same principle, and that Strumilin's 'surplus product' was included in the prices of capital goods and consumer goods alike at the same *quasi*-profit rate. The reason is that under these circumstances the investment of the profits of enterprises in sector 2 in purchasing capital goods would tend to bid up the prices of the latter until enterprises in sector 1 were earning profits on a comparable scale to those in the other sector. From thenceforth investment could be expected to occur in both sectors so as to expand their output capacities at approximately equal rates; although a system of this type would be inherently unstable and in danger of cumulative inflation (or its opposite); any change in investment bringing a change in prices and profits to reinforce the initial change. Implied in this uniformity of the sector price-levels would be that our two macro-price-ratios when defined in the *second* of the two senses we have just mentioned would be equal if (but of course only if) the average labour-capital ratio were the same in both sectors; any difference in the price-levels in the sense of a different ratio of s to w being due to differences in the capital-labour ratio.

This is, however, to assume the conditions of capitalist competition that give rise to a tendency towards an equal profit-rate. In the absence of these conditions there would seem to be no need for a uniformity of the price-levels of the two sectors. If, for example, funds for investment were channelled through the State Budget so that both total investment and its distribution between the sectors were effectively planned, our two macro-price-ratios in the relevant sense could diverge, even if the average capital-labour ratio happened to be uniform; each of them being severally determined by the factors we have mentioned.

Is there anything to be said in favour of having uniform price-levels even when investment and its distribution between the sectors is centrally planned? Contrary to an earlier opinion of the present writer,* this question has to be answered in the affirmative, and for a reason that is implied by the argument of previous chapters. This reason immediately appears if we consider the price-relations needed to induce enterprises to choose an optimum technique in the light of the criterion we discussed in Chapters III and IV.

In Chapter IV we saw that the optimum degree of capital intensity in sector 2 was reached when the proportional increase in cost of choosing a capital good of higher productivity was equal to the proportional increase of productivity multiplied by a factor $(s+w)/s$. We noted that this factor represents the magnitude of the percentage increase in s per worker employed (or per wage-unit expended in current production) for every percentage rise in productivity, i.e. $\frac{ds}{s} = \frac{dp_c}{p_c} \cdot \frac{s+w}{s}$. Thus if the ratio of profit to wage-bill for an enterprise were the same as the ratio s/w from a social point of view, the enterprise would then find that its profit was maximized for a given investment-expenditure if it moved along the curve of alternative types of technique to the point where the percentage cost-difference exceeded the percentage gain in productivity by the amount of the above-mentioned factor.

Since for purpose of this choice it is the *proportional* cost-difference that matters, the price-*level* of sector 1 products

* Expressed in an earlier draft of this chapter; also in an article in *Soviet Studies*, vol. ix, no. 2, p. 139.

(capital goods), whether based on wage-cost alone or raised above this, might seem to be of no importance. If, however, an analogous choice of technique is to be made by enterprises in sector 1 itself, then an analogous situation must apply to them: the choice that is most profitable for them to make must be (in what we called the 'normal case' in Chapter IV)* where the percentage cost-difference exceeds the percentage productivity-gain by the same factor $(s+w)/s$. For this to be the case the selling price of output must exceed its wage-cost sufficiently to make the difference between them as a ratio to the wage-cost equal to s/w; and this would mean that the latter ratio was uniformly applied to the two sectors.

If, however, the major part of s, instead of accruing to the enterprise, were to be diverted directly into the Budget by a Turnover Tax (as was described above), then the ratio s'/w (as we may write it) appropriate to the *enterprise* would be an equivalently smaller one; and consequently the factor $(s'+w)/s'$ appropriate to it would be larger. If its selling-price is fixed so as to yield no more than a narrow profit-margin over its 'planned cost', a quite small proportional rise in productivity will suffice to augment this profit-margin by a large proportional amount. Consequently a premium will be placed on choosing methods of production of very high capital-intensity—much higher than the optimum according to our criterion in Chapter IV.

This *penchant* on the part of enterprises for too-expensive capital goods could be combatted by measures designed to widen the price-differential between alternative types of capital goods so as to make price-differences greater than differences in their respective labour-costs. This might be done, for example, by a *flat-rate* subsidy to such goods so as to reduce their selling

* In the case considered there where p_m is appreciably *lower* than p_i and the cost-difference needs to exceed the productivity difference by *less* than $(s+w)/s$, the ratio of capital to labour used in branch-i is equivalently *above* the average (despite our assumption of fixed proportions) by reason of the relatively large amount of labour embodied in m-products and used in conjunction with a given amount of L_i. If our principle for applying any *agio* in the price of capital goods were applied here, namely that this *agio* should be related to the amount of capital employed, the price-level of i-products and hence the appropriate s/w would be equivalently raised in this case.

prices below their costs,* or alternatively by applying to them in the form of a tax a positive *agio* which, instead of being uniform, was progressively graduated against those of higher cost. Both of these would in different ways conflict with the aims which we envisaged above as being served by an *agio* in the price of capital goods. An easier as well as a less objectionable way of achieving the desired end would be to replace the Turnover Tax by a percentage tax on the profits of enterprises.† Since an enterprise would maximize its own retained profit *post*-tax by maximizing total profit *pre*-tax, and since the latter would measure (approximately, at least) what was *s* from the standpoint of the system as a whole,‡ this should give the enterprise a bias towards the socially desirable technique. An offsetting disadvantage might be that, in so far as it enabled extra profits to be more easily won (as it would tend to do unless the percentage rate of tax was very high) it would weaken the incentive to cost-reduction by other methods: i.e. methods unconnected with choice of technique or with the substitution of one capital good by another. But such a disadvantage seems likely to weigh less heavily in the balance than the advantage to be gained from preventing wasteful use of the investment potential of the economy.

This sort of price-relationship would be appropriate to the kind of growth-process of which we were speaking in Chapter III and (in the main) in Chapter IV. It does not follow that it would be appropriate to all types of growth-process. It would scarcely be so for what we called at the end of Chapter IV a circular m_2 process; which would seem to require a relatively low price-level for at least certain categories of capital goods (i.e. m_2 products). Nor would it apparently be suited to the type

* For example, suppose two types of capital goods cost respectively 100 and 105, the cost of the second being greater by 5 per cent than that of the first. Then a flat-rate subsidy of 50 to each would enable them to be sold at 50 and 55—a price difference of 10 per cent.

† A proposal, indeed, made by Strumilin in the course of advocating a uniform price-level for the two sectors (S. Strumilin, 'The Question of Calculating the Value of Output' in *Voprosi Ekonomiki*, 1956, no. 12, pp. 96–100).

‡ It should be noted that the relevant *s* here is that which is a function solely of the rate of investment (as in our model). In so far as the surplus product of the consumer goods sector is raised by the amount of 'social consumption', *this* part of the difference between retail price and cost should be covered by a Turnover Tax (as was also proposed by Strumilin) and not by a tax on profits, and should *not* reappear in the *s/w* appropriate to the capital goods sector.

of development that was considered in Chapter V, which again might seem to require different prices for capital goods of different destinations. Such types of development cannot, however, cover more than a certain period or phase in the growth of an economy, for the reasons we noticed; and accordingly a pattern of 'uniform price-levels' for the sectors could be regarded, perhaps, as the macro-price-relation appropriate to a 'normal' (or possibly 'later') phase of development.

To recapitulate, we seem to have reached two conclusions of some consequence: (a) that the inclusion of an *agio* in the price of capital goods is to be looked at, not only as a means of adjusting the relative *costs* of capital goods to the users of them, but even more as a means of appropriately adjusting the incentive to the *using* enterprise when faced with alternative methods of production of differing productivity; (b) that in the 'normal case' this *agio* should be derived from the s/w ratio prevailing in the consumer goods sector, as defined by the second of our two macro-price relations (in the 'non-normal' case this ratio being adjusted up or down according to divergences of the proportion of capital to labour from the average as measured by the ratios of L in the different branches).

The point which we have been making could be looked at, alternatively, in this way. With a given investment fund to be expended,* the choice between different technical forms (of varying degrees of capital intensity) will be between different product-totals (e.g., per annum) at different wage-costs. The advantage to an enterprise of the more capital-intensive form consists essentially in the economy in current wage-cost that it yields. But any comparison of this difference in wage-cost with the difference in product necessarily depends on the level at which the price of the product stands relatively to the wage. At one extreme, where the price of the product of a day's labour is equal to a day's wage, any labour-saving, however small, must appear as an advantage (i.e., so long as productivity is raised at all by choosing a more capital-intensive form of technique). As one recedes from this extreme, and the product-price

---

* If one prefers to think in terms of *adding* to existing investment outlays, then the relevant consideration will be the additional *net* product resulting from the additional expenditure, and the size of this *net* product in price-terms will depend on the product-price relatively to the wage. Cf. Joan Robinson, *op. cit.*, pp. 106–8.

is raised compared with the wage, the margin of advantage will come at an earlier point in the transition to capital-intensity, where a larger degree of labour-saving is involved; until in the limit the degree of economy in wage-cost becomes a negligible consideration compared with the difference in total product. Thus by adjusting a product's selling price as paid to the enterprise, relatively to its wage-cost, the choice of technique by the enterprise can be adjusted in any required degree. But only if the relation of this price to the wage is the same as that which in the consumer goods sector is a measure of the rate of investment will choice of technique be consistent with that rate of investment, in the sense of maximizing the growth-rate that such a rate of investment can yield.

A possible objection which may spring to mind is that we are now talking about *price*-relations whereas in earlier chapters our analysis was conducted in terms of *real* relations (i.e. of products and of labour). Can we be sure that the former remain the same and can be treated as playing the same rôle as the latter? To show the connection between the two, it may be as well to set out the main equations defining the price-relations, using the same categories and notation as were employed in Chapters III and IV (but using in this case a large S and a large W, indicating that these represent totals, and writing c, i and m as subscripts to S and W to indicate the sector or branch to which the latter refer).

Let us start from the assumption that the ratio s/w in *price-terms* is applied uniformly to all branches (as in the 'normal case' we have just been considering) namely:

$$\frac{S_c}{W_c} = \frac{S_i}{W_i} = \frac{S_{m1}}{W_{m1}} = \frac{S_{m2}}{W_{m2}}.$$

From what we have said above about our second macro-price relation it is clear that the following equality must hold:

$$\frac{W_i + W_{m1+2}}{W_c} = \frac{S_c}{W_c}.$$

By analogy with the argument of Chapter IV (as applied to the 'normal case' with uniform p's), we may presume that

$$\frac{W_i}{W_c} = \frac{S_c}{W_c + S_c}.$$

It follows (since $S_i/W_i = S_c/W_c$) that

$$\frac{W_i + S_i}{W_c + S_c} = \frac{S_c}{W_c + S_c}.$$

Therefore $W_i + S_i = S_c$; *i.e.* the total output of branch-i of sector 1 is equal in price-terms to the surplus of the consumer goods sector.

It can similarly be shown that the output of branch-m_1 is equal to the surplus of branch-i, namely:

$$W_{m1} + S_{m1} = S_i$$

and also the output of branch-m_2 is equal to the combined surplus of m_1 and m_2, namely:

$$W_{m2} + S_{m2} = S_{m1} + S_{m2}$$

from which, incidentally, it follows that

$$S_{m1} = W_{m2}; \text{ also } S_i = W_{m1+2}$$

What remains to be shown is that S_c/W_c (and hence $S_c/(W_c + S_c)$) is the same in price-terms as it is in real terms. This can be done quite easily. Our statement of the second macro-price relation* has defined S_c/W_c in price terms as being equal to the ratio of the wage-bill of the investment sector to the wage-bill of the consumer goods sector. If wages are uniform between the two sectors, it follows that this ratio must be the same as the ratio between the *labour force* of the two sectors, namely:

$$\frac{S_c}{W_c} = \frac{W_i + W_{m1+2}}{W_c} = \frac{L_i + L_{m1+2}}{L_c}.$$

Summarizing (and writing P with appropriate subscript for the total output of a sector or branch multiplied by its appropriate price-level), we have:

* i.e., in its initial formulation, before introducing the complication of so-called 'social consumption'.

$$P_c = W_c + W_i + W_{m1+2}$$
$$S_c = W_i + W_{m1+2}$$
$$P_i = S_c$$
$$P_{m1} = S_i$$
$$P_{m2} = S_{m1+2}$$

$$\frac{P_i + P_{m1+2}}{P_c} = \frac{S_c + S_i + S_{m1+2}}{W_c + W_i + W_{m1+2}} = \frac{S_c}{W_c} = \frac{L_i + L_{m1+2}}{L_c}.$$

At first glance it might seem that to raise the price-level of sector 1 (i.e. to make $P_i/W_i = P_c/W_c$) must inevitably result in a change in the s/w ratio in the consumer goods sector by raising the cost of products sold to it by sector 1 and thence affecting either the prices of consumer goods or the size of s. This, however, will not be the case. With a given rate of investment, as defined by the ratio of employment in the two sectors, and a given level of money wages, the price-level of consumer goods can only change with a change in productivity (p_c).* What a rise in the price of i-products will do is to lower both consumer goods prices and s as a ratio to their production cost (including in the latter the cost of i-products as well as the wages of those employed in this sector); but to leave both prices of consumer goods and s unchanged as a ratio to w.

It should, perhaps, be stressed once more that the importance of such considerations as these will depend on the extent to which investment and its allocation, while planned in the *main*, is *incompletely* planned, and there remains accordingly a margin within which enterprises can influence or adapt these plans and supplement them from their own resources (in which case their decisions are likely to be influenced by the price-structure). They will also have some importance to the extent that planning is guided by indices, such as a coefficient of effectiveness of investment, that are expressed in price-terms. It is unlikely that any actual situation will correspond completely to either of the

---

* If we hold to the assumption of our earlier model that any rise in p_c will lead to an increase in the rate of investment (in the degree to which s/w is raised), then the price of consumer goods must remain constant and s/w will rise alike in money and in real terms. But if investment does not increase, the price of consumer goods must fall, thereby raising real wages and leaving s/w unchanged.

two extremes, wholly centralized or wholly decentralized. *Some*
discretion is bound to be allowed to the enterprise, or at any
rate tolerated in practice. The line between new investment and
replacement is not easily drawn (*vide* the familiar example of
replacing old plant by more modern plant of greater productive
capacity), nor is that between replacement and current maintenance and repair. Not all capital goods can be distributed by
centralized allocations; and in small or large degree there is
bound to be decentralization in the ordering of supplies on a
contractual basis. To the extent that this is so, the transfer of
capital goods from producing to using enterprise becomes a
quasi-market process, and capital goods acquire the character
of '*quasi*-commodities' (to use Professor Lange's convenient
phrase). Hence the need for an appropriate adjustment of price-
levels. It would be too much to expect such adjustments to be
made with complete consistency: the most one could expect
would be the correction of pronounced (and harmful) inconsistencies and of any pronounced tendency for 'profitability' to
the enterprise to pull against the main objectives of investment-
policy, and in particular to distort the investment-pattern as
regards choice of technique and allocation between sectors. It
has to be remembered, however, that any considerable move in
the direction of autonomy of the enterprise in investment decisions is likely to conflict in some measure with the needs of
growth in ways that even a well-articulated price-system may
be incapable of preventing; and in any compromise between
planning and market this is likely to be the crucial and decisive
issue on which the answer will turn.

To the purist, of course, no such compromise would be ac-
ceptable, since at this or that point price-relations would depart
from the theoretical ideal. But the standpoint of purists in such
matters is coming today to be recognized as being *simpliste* to
the point of being a little absurd. In the first place, can anyone
seriously claim, after all that has been said and written about
welfare *optima* in the past two decades, that an 'ideal' allocation
of resources can be theoretically defined with any approach to
precision? Secondly, even if it could be, does anyone seriously
believe that any price-system which could be practically devised
would be capable of attaining an ideal position without a quite
sizeable margin of error? In discussing such matters 'western'

economists might do well to remember Mr. Little's blunt warning: "Economic welfare is a subject in which rigour and refinement are probably worse than useless. Rough theory, or good common sense, is, in practice, what we require."*

* I. M. D. Little, *A Critique of Welfare Economics*, Oxford 1957, p. 279.

APPENDIX

BY

L. JOHANSEN & A. GHOSH

(A) NOTES TO CHAPTER III

WE shall investigate the relationships between the variables introduced above in Chapter III under two different assumptions:

   A. That the technique chosen at a certain point of time can only
   be applied in connection with capital equipment accumulated
   after this point of time.
   B. That the technique chosen can be applied in connection with
   the total stock of capital.

The former case would seem to be the more realistic one. We shall
see, however, that we obtain quite similar conclusions on both
assumptions.

Case A.

Let there be initially an employment $L_i(0)$ and $L_c(0)$ in the two
sectors, the workers constituting $L_i(0)$ being supported by the surplus
of consumption goods produced in the c-sector by the workers constituting $L_c(0)$. At a point of time $t > 0$ the employment in the
i-sector has got the addition $L_i(t) - L_i(0)$. These workers have
to be supported by the additional employment $L_c(t) - L_c(0)$ in the
c-sector. This condition yields the relationship

$$(1) \qquad [L_i - L_i(0)] \, w = [L_c - L_c(0)] \, (p_c - w)$$

where we for the sake of brevity have omitted the t. $(p_c - w)$ is
assumed throughout to be positive.

The number of units of capital equipment produced by the
i-sector per unit of time is $p_i L_i$. Assuming that each worker in
the c-sector has to be equipped with one unit of capital, this gives
rise to the following condition

$$(2) \qquad \frac{dL_c}{dt} = p_i L_i .$$

Equations (1) and (2) are valid for $t \geq 0$ only, and p_i and p represent the technique chosen at the point of time $t = 0$ for the foreseeable future. Assuming that the workers $L_c(0)$ continue to support the workers $L_i(0)$ in the future as they did at $t = 0$, we need not worry about how they are equipped and we can apply p_c to the labour force $L_c - L_c(0)$ only. In (2) we can apply p_i to the total L_i since the workers in the i-sector are not equipped with any capital.

Equations (1) and (2) yield the following solution for the total employment

$$(3) \qquad L(t) = L_i(t) + L_c(t) = L_i(0) \frac{p_c}{p_c - w} e^{\frac{p_i(p_c - w)}{w} t} + \left[L_c(0) - \frac{w}{p_c - w} L_i(0) \right] .$$

Within the range of possible development objectives we shall now contrast the two extremes: (1) The very short run point of view and (2) the very long run point of view. We shall assume that the choice of p_i and p_c are restricted by a relationship

$$(4) \qquad \frac{1}{p_i} = f(p_c)$$

The function f can be interpreted as a kind of cost function, relating the cost (measured in man-hours or man-years) of producing one unit of capital equipment $(1/p_i)$ to the productivity of the capital (when manned with one worker) in the c-sector. We assume

$$(5) \qquad \frac{df}{dp_c} = f'(p_c) > 0, \quad \frac{d^2f}{dp_c{}^2} = f''(p_c) > 0.$$

The very short run point of view. From the short run point of view we should like to maximize total employment immediately. However, $L_i(0) + L_c(0)$ is given independently of our (p_i, p_c) – choice. $L_c(0)$ is given by the existing capital equipment and $L_i(0)$ is given by the current surplus produced by the existing employment in the c-sector. (We consider the wage rate as given.) This being so, it is most natural to consider the immediate rate of increase in total employment, which means to consider $dL(t)/dt$ for $t = 0$. This magnitude is easily derived from (3). We get

$$(6) \qquad \frac{dL}{dt} = L_i(0) \ \frac{p_i p_c}{w} \ \text{(for } t = 0).$$

This means that in order to maximize the immediate rate of increase in total employment we should maximize the composite productivity $p_i p_c$. Doing this under condition (4) yields the result

$$(7) \qquad f'(p_c) \frac{p_c}{f(p_c)} = 1.$$

This means we should choose the productivity p_c which corresponds to the point on the cost curve $f(p_c)$ where its elasticity equals unity (provided that such a point exists). The latter assumption in (5) secures that the second order condition of maximum is fulfilled.

The very long run point of view. In the very long run it is obvious that the exponential term in (3) will dominate, the exponent being positive. Accepting a very long run point of view as a basis for our choice means therefore to maximize the exponent

$$(8) \qquad g = \frac{p_i(p_c - w)}{w}$$

which yields the condition

$$(9) \qquad f'(p_c) \frac{p_c}{f(p_c)} = \frac{p_c}{p_c - w}.$$

This says that we should now choose a value of p_c corresponding to a point on the cost curve $f(p_c)$ where its elasticity is greater than unity (provided that such a point exists) rather than equal to unity as in the former case. Also in this case $f''(p_c) > 0$ secures that the second order condition of maximum is satisfied.

In order to compare the solutions (7) and (9) and to see how the solution (9) depends on the wage rate, let the value of p_c determined by (9) be denoted by $p_c(w)$. We then see that the solution (7) is equal to $p_c(0)$, which means that if the wage rate were equal to zero the short and the long run points of view would produce identical results.

By implicit differentiation in equation (9) we get the following expression for the dependence of p_c on w when we accept the long run point of view:

(10) $$\frac{dp_c(w)}{dw} = \frac{f'(p_c)}{f''(p_c)(p_c - w)}$$

which is positive under the conditions (5). This means that the higher the given wage rate, the greater is the optimal productivity in the c-sector.

As a corollary this implies that if $w > 0$ the optimal p_c from a long run point of view is greater than the optimal p_c from a short run point of view.

Case B.

We now assume that the technique chosen can be projected into the old capital as well as the new one. To make the reasoning clear we can for instance suppose that there exists a kind of 'world market' where we can exchange our old machines for others embodying the technology we choose. Alternatively we could think of our initial capital as held in monetary form so that we can choose what kind of equipment we want to buy for it on 'the world market'.

In this case we need not distinguish between the initially employed workers and the additionally employed ones as we did in equation (1). Instead of (1) we therefore now write

(11) $$L_i w = L_c(p_c - w).$$

Equation (2) still holds in its original form.

For total employment we now get the solution

(12) $$L(t) = L_c(0) \frac{p_c}{w} e^{\frac{p_i(p_c - w)}{w} t}$$

where $L_c(0)$ is the initial employment in the c-sector. In contrast to case A, $L_c(0)$ is, however, not given. By choosing what concrete shape to give our capital stock, we can choose the magnitude of $L_c(0)$.

Assume that the value of our initial capital stock is $K(0)$. We then consider $K(0)$ as a given datum. Assuming as before that we have one capital unit per man, $L_c(0)$ will be the number of capital units in which we embody the value of our initial capital. Assuming further that the capital units are valued according to their labour cost, we have

(13) $$K(\text{o}) = f(p_c)L_c(\text{o})$$

where $f(p_c)$ is the cost function introduced by (4). Equations (4) and (13) now describe the possible choices of p_i, p_c and $L_c(\text{o})$: we can choose any set of these magnitudes which satisfy (4) and (13) for the given value of $K(\text{o})$. We can then write (12) as

(14) $$L(t) = K(\text{o}) \frac{p_i p_c}{w} e^{\frac{p_i(p_c - w)}{w}t}$$

Let us now again consider the very short run and the very long run points of view as we did in case A.

The very short run point of view.

In the case which we are now considering it is possible to influence $L(\text{o})$ directly, and from the short run point of view we therefore want to maximize this magnitude. From (14) we see that

(15) $$L(\text{o}) = K(\text{o}) \frac{p_i p_c}{w}$$

Since $K(\text{o})$ and w are given, this implies that we should select p and p_c in such a way as to maximize the product $p_i p_c$ subject to the constraint (4). Even though the situation is now somewhat different from what it was in case A, we thus get exactly the same rule as we did in that case for choosing the p's.

The very long run point of view.

It is immediately clear that we also from this point of view get the same rule for the choice of the p's as we did in case A, since the growth rate in (14) is the same as the exponent in the solution (3).

In the diagrams below are shown two members of the family of time curves for total employment between which we have to choose in each of the cases A and B.

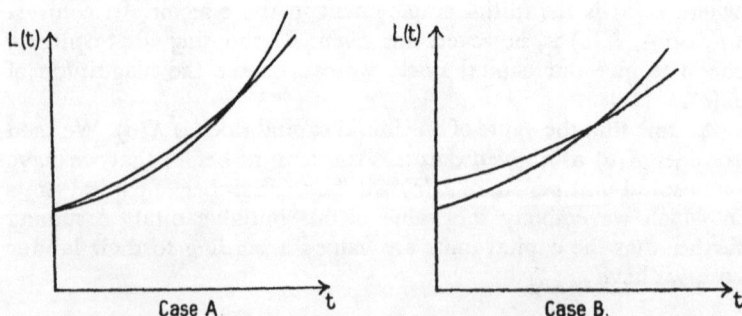

Case A

Case B.

In case A both curves start at the same point, but with different slopes. In case B they start from different points.

WE base our analysis in what follows on a similar assumption to that of case A in the Note to Chapter III. Corresponding to equation (1) there we now have:

$$(1) \qquad (l_i + l_{m1} + l_{m2})\, w = l_c(p_c - w)$$

where we have introduced the notation

$$l_c = L_c(t) - L_c(0), \text{ etc.}$$

For the increase in the employment in the c-sector, we have now to consider two terms. First, the newly employed workers in the i-sector (l_i) will produce $p_i l_i$ capital units per unit of time, each of which is capable of employing one worker in the c-sector. Secondly, the previously employed workers in the i-sector ($L_i(0)$) are capable of producing some capital units for the c-sector. Let us denote this flow of capital units by N_i. If some equipment for the c-sector is produced by workers and equipment transferred from the m-sector to the i-sector at $t = 0$, N_i also includes this. N_i is likely to decrease with p_c. More generally we can say that N_i depends also on how different the capital equipment wanted for the c-sector subsequently to the date $t = 0$ is from what was produced previously, and if there is a difference, on how rigid the production structure is. If there were complete rigidity, and we wanted a p_c from $t = 0$ onward that was different from what it previously had been, N would equal zero.

The above arguments give rise to

$$(2) \qquad \frac{dl_c}{dt} = p_i l_i + N_i.$$

In an exactly similar way we have

$$(3) \qquad \frac{dl_i}{dt} = p_m l_{m1} + N_{m1}$$

and

$$(4) \qquad \frac{dl_{m1}}{dt} + \frac{dl_{m2}}{dt} = p_m l_{m2} + N_{m2}$$

where N_{m1} and N_{m2} are to be interpreted in a similar way to N in (2). By existing equipment and employment we assume that we can produce $N_m = N_{m1} + N_{m2}$ units of machine-tools. Of these N_{m1} are allocated to the i-sector and N_{m2} to the m-sector itself, so that $N_{m1} + N_{m2} = N_m$.

By successive eliminations the system (1)–(4) produces a first order differential equation for l_{m2} with the solution

$$(5) \qquad l_{m2} = \frac{N_{m2}}{p_m}(e^{Gt} - 1)$$

where the exponent G is given by

$$(6) \qquad G = \frac{p_m p_i (p_c - w)}{p_m w + p_i (p_c - w)}.$$

By 'backward insertions' we then obtain the solution for the other variables. First we obtain the solution for l_{m1}. Adding this to (5) we obtain for the employment in the m-sector

$$(7) \qquad l_m = l_{m1} + l_{m2} = \frac{N_{m2}}{G}(e^{Gt} - 1).$$

By further insertions and integrations we obtain the following not very convenient expression for the total employment (above the initial employment):

$$(8) \qquad l = l_m + l_i + l_c$$

$$= \frac{N_{m2}}{G}\left[1 + \left(\frac{p_i}{G} + 1\right)\left(\frac{p_m}{G} - 1\right)\right](e^{Gt} - 1)$$

$$+ \tfrac{1}{2}p_i\left[N_{m1} - N_{m2}\left(\frac{p_m}{G} - 1\right)\right]t^2$$

$$+ \left[N_{m1} + N_i - N_{m2}\left(\frac{p_i}{G} + 1\right)\left(\frac{p_m}{G} - 1\right)\right]t.$$

Let us first consider the contributions of the elements N_i, N_{m1} and N_{m2} to solution (8). We see that N_i contributes only to the linear term in (8), which is the least powerful term in the long run. N_{m1} contributes to the more powerful quadratic term in (8), while only N_{m2} contributes to the most powerful exponential term. This is important when we shall contrast short run and long run policies by means of the formula.

Before doing so we shall try to depict the range of choice open to the planner in the present model. Let us first consider the productivities p_m, p_i and p_c.

Productivity in the m-sector is completely determined within this sector itself, since the m-sector is not dependent on any equipment from other sectors. Further it is reasonable to assume that the more efficient a machine-tool is in producing machine-tools, the more efficient is it also in its alternative use in the i-sector. There seems then to be no economic reason why p_m should not be made as large as technology permits. The above arguments are valid only when we disregard the period of production. If a greater p_m requires a longer period of production, some economic considerations are necessary to determine p_m. Furthermore, some economic considerations would enter in connection with the production of machine tools by means of old equipment. However, for the following discussion it is not necessary to go deeper into this.

For p_i and p_c the situation is different. In the first place they may depend on p_m. This is, however, irrelevant in cases where p_m can be considered as a given datum for reasons as those given above. But we shall have a similar connection between p_i and p_c as we had in Chapter III. We write it as we did there

$$(9) \qquad \frac{1}{p_i} = f(p_c) \text{ where } f'(p_c) > 0 \text{ and } f''(p_c) > 0.$$

It is no longer so easy to interpret this relation as a cost function, since both labour and capital are involved in producing the equipment used in the c-sector. (9) says, however, that the more tractors (say) we produce per man-year in the i-sector (with tools of a kind determined through the determination of p_m), the less productive will each tractor (operated by one man) be.

We shall not write down explicitly any formula which expresses technological restrictions on the choice of the values of N_{m1}, N_{m2} and N_i. We shall only repeat that they are restricted by the degree to which we are able to use existing equipment to produce equipment of the kind we want from point of time $t = 0$. They will therefore depend on the flexibility of existing equipment, and on what kind of equipment—i.e. what values of p_m, p_i and p_c—we choose.

The N's can, however, not be chosen freely within the range given by technological considerations alone. Equation (1) imposes the two following requirements upon their values:

$$(10) \qquad N_m = N_{m1} + N_{m2} = \frac{p_c - w}{w} N_i$$

$$(11) \qquad p_m N_{m2} = p_i \frac{p_c - w}{w} N_{m1}.$$

To bring about the balance (11) should not be hampered by technological conditions, since N_{m2} and N_{m1} represent only different allocations of the same kind of output. To satisfy (10) may be more difficult since it may in certain situations require a transfer of equipment from one sector to another. Even this should, however, not be impossible when both the m-sector and the i-sector use the same kind of machine-tools.

Let us now see what the solution (8) implies from the very short and the very long run point of view.

The very short run point of view. Since the total employment at point of time $t = 0$ is given by the existing equipment, we consider the growth rate of employment. From (8) we derive

$$(12) \qquad \frac{dL}{dt} = \frac{dl}{dt} = N_m + N_i \qquad \text{(for } t = 0\text{)},$$

which is also obvious from equations (2)–(4), since all the l's equal zero at $t = 0$. Taking now into account the requirement (10), we can write (12) as

$$(13) \qquad \frac{dL}{dt} = \frac{p_c N_i}{w} \qquad \text{(for } t = 0\text{)}.$$

The objective of maximizing immediately the growth rate of total employment therefore implies to maximize the product $p_c N_i$, which means to expand immediately as fast as possible the 'wage fund' of consumption goods through production of 'tractors' by means of existing equipment. In maximizing $p_c N_i$ we must take into account that N_i depends on p_c as pointed out above. We then notice that the solution obtained here reminds one of the solution obtained in Chapter III where we should maximize $p_c p_i$.

The very long run point of view. In the long run the exponential term in (8) will dominate the other terms. Since (what is easy to demonstrate) the square bracket in front of the term $(e^{Gt} - 1)$ is always positive, a policy which aims at the greatest possible achievement in the very long run should therefore maximize the exponent G. In this maximization we can first maximize p_m independently of p_c and p_i for reasons indicated above. It is then illustrative to write the growth rate as

$$(14) \qquad G = \frac{p_m}{p_m \dfrac{w}{p_i(p_c - w)} + 1}$$

which shows that the rest of the problem is equivalent to maximizing the expression $p_i(p_c - w)$. The long-run policy leads therefore to a maximization problem which is formally very similar to the one we obtained in Chapter III.

It is interesting to observe that

$$(15) \qquad G < p_m \qquad \text{if } w > 0$$

and

$$(16) \qquad G \to p_m \qquad \text{if } w \to 0.$$

This means that the exponent G in (8) is always less than p_m if the wage rate w is positive. If the wage rate approaches zero G approaches p_m. G being the asymptotic (relative) growth rate of total employment, we can therefore say that the lower is the wage rate, the more important is the machine-building industry for determining the long run growth rate of total employment, and the nearer is this growth rate to the self-regenerating power of this industry taken by itself.

Remark on equation (4).

Consider a break-down of industry m_2 into a sequence m_{21}, m_{22}, . . ., $m_{2,j\text{-}1}$, m_{2j}, . . . such that m_{2j} produces machine-tools for sector $m_{2,j\text{-}1}$, and, in particular, m_{21} produces tools for m_1. We should then have (provided the productivities are the same in all subsectors)

$$\frac{dl_{m1}}{dt} = p_m l_{m21} + N_{m21}$$

$$\frac{dl_{m21}}{dt} = p_m l_{m22} + N_{m22}$$

$$(17) \qquad\qquad \vdots$$

$$\frac{dl_{m2,j\text{-}1}}{dt} = p_m l_{m2j} + N_{m2j}$$

$$\vdots$$

where the symbols are interpreted analogously with previous notations.

Defining now

(18) $$l_{m2} = \sum_{j=1}^{\infty} l_{m2j} \,, \quad N_{m2} = \sum_{j=1}^{\infty} N_{m2j}$$

we obtain equation (4) by summation of the above equations for the subsectors. This shows the equivalence between equation (4) in this note and some arguments in the text based on the conception of a sequence of industries as defined above.

INDEX

84 n.; tendency to equal rate of, 95

Railway, electrification of (as example), 23 n.; double and single track (as example), 24; Research Institute, U.S.S.R., 25; development in N. America, 74

Ramsey, Frank P., 18, 19–20

Recoupment, period of, 23–5

Redundancy, of plant, 9, 63

Reserve, of labour, 32, 62–3

Ricardo, David, 40

Robertson, Professor Sir Dennis H., 19, 20 n., 92 n.

Robinson, Mrs. Joan V., 1 n., 52, 91 n., 98 n.

Rostow, Professor Walt W., 74 n.

Roumania, 84 n.

Savings, and investment, 2–3; defined, 3; decisions of individuals, 17–18; ratio, 14, 33, 35, 42, 67, 73

Schumpeterian *entrepreneurs*, 74

Scitovszky, Professor Tibor de (sometimes spelled Scitovsky), 6 n., 8 n.

Sen, Dr. Amartya Kumar, 17, 18, 37, 42 n., 60 n.

Singer, Dr. H. W., 33 n.

Smith, Adam, 40

'Social consumption', 93, 97 n.

Socialism, and capitalism contrasted, 2–12, 74–5, 76; and production for use, 27; price-policy under, 77 *seq.*; 'first period of', 78, *see also* Socialist countries, Planning

Socialist countries, growth-rates of, 1; recent discussions in, 77 *seq.*, *see also under individual countries*

Soviet economists, and calculation of 'effectiveness of investment', 23–7; discuss law of value and price-policy, 78 *seq.*

Soviet Union, difference of sector price-levels in, 25; in the '20's, 30; First Five Year Plan and after, 70;

growth-rate in, 70; position of enterprises in, 81

Stalin, Joseph, 78

Stationary state, 63

Strumilin, Academician S. G., 25 n., 26–7, 79 *and* n., 93, 94, 97 n.

Subsistence, fund, 29, 48; economy, 32, *see also* Wages

Surplus, marketed, of agriculture, 29–30; of consumer goods as an investment determinant, 29 *seq.*, 36–9; product, 93, 94; as an equal ratio to wages in both sectors, 96–101, *see also* 'Compounding effect'

'Take-off', into industrial growth, 73, 74 n.

Taxes, on profit, 3 n., 85, 93, 97; on turnover, 3 n., 25, 83, 89, 90, 93, 96, 97; on agriculture, 30

Technical coefficient, 36, 47 n., 48, 50, 96 n.

Technical innovation, 63, 70, 71, 83

Technique, choice of, 23, 33 *seq.*, 52 *seq.*, 68, 95–8, 104 *seq.*

'Textiles first', 74

Time, investment decisions involving, 15 *seq.*, 24, 44–6; individual choices over, irrational, 18

Time-horizon, 13, 62, 71

Time-lags, 45, 47, 63 n.

Time-preference (or discount), 5, 15 *seq.*

Tinbergen, Professor J., 17, 19 n.

Tolkachi, 80

Uncertainty, 7, 17–18, 75; 'secondary', 8, 10; 'individualist', 8 n.

Underdeveloped countries, investment policy of, 2, 33 *seq.*; balanced growth in, 6, 12; arrested growth in, 8, 73–4; reserve of labour in, 32; agriculture in, 29–30; development limited by capital goods industry, 65

Unemployment, 'disguised', 32 and n.

MONTHLY REVIEW

an independent socialist magazine
edited by Paul M. Sweezy and Harry Magdoff

Business Week: ". . . a brand of socialism that is thorough-going and tough-minded, drastic enough to provide the sharp break with the past that many left-wingers in the underdeveloped countries see as essential. At the same time they maintain a sturdy independence of both Moscow and Peking that appeals to neutralists. And their skill in manipulating the abstruse concepts of modern economics impresses would-be intellectuals. . . . Their analysis of the troubles of capitalism is just plausible enough to be disturbing."

Bertrand Russell: "Your journal has been of the greatest interest to me over a period of time. I am not a Marxist by any means as I have sought to show in critiques published in several books, but I recognize the power of much of your own analysis and where I disagree I find your journal valuable and of stimulating importance. I want to thank you for your work and to tell you of my appreciation of it."

The Wellesley Department of Economics: " . . . the leading Marxist intellectual (not Communist) economic journal published anywhere in the world, and is on our subscription list at the College library for good reasons."

Albert Einstein: "Clarity about the aims and problems of socialism is of greatest significance in our age of transition. . . . I consider the founding of this magazine to be an important public service." (In his article, "Why Socialism" in Vol. I, No. 1.)

DOMESTIC: $7 for one year, $12 for two years, $5 for one-year student subscription.
FOREIGN: $8 for one year, $14 for two years, $6 for one-year student subscription. (Subscription rates subject to change.)

116 West 14th Street, New York, New York 10011

www.ingramcontent.com/pod-product-compliance
Lightning Source LLC
Chambersburg PA
CBHW032149020426
42334CB00016B/1248